Steve Larkin is a poet, singer songcomedic host and impresario ren
entertaining live work.

A former International Poetry Slam
Poetry nominee Steve is the founder and chief of Hammer & Tongue
- the UK's leading poetry slam organisation that has led the charge
of poetry back to the Royal Albert Hall. Steve is the creator of two
critically acclaimed spoken word theatre shows: N.O.N.C.E. and TES,
the front to 'world-folk-punk-skiffle' band Inflatable Buddha, a musician
in his own right, and a poet whose career has spanned three decades
and involved performing world-over in diverse venues to diverse
audiences, from convicted violent criminals in a high security prison to
MPs at the Houses of Parliament.

Press Clippings:

"Steve Larkin is a poet-philosopher disguised as a club entertainer.
Lacing profundity with profanities, deep tracks with cheap gags,
he weaves comedy, politics and style to leave audiences laughing
thoughtful and infected." Jim Thomas

"Electrifying fusion of music and the spoken word...affability and quick,
biting wit with the social conscience of Pete Seeger" ***** Victoria
Times Colonist

"Superb spoken-word - essential viewing" ***** Fringe Guru

"Prepare to be stunned and inspired by the power of Larkin's spoken
word." ***** Edmonton Sun, Canada

"Part philosophy, part hysterically funny humour" Nightshift Magazine

"Steve Larkin, has the facial expressions of Vic Reeves, and often, the
blunt quick-wittedness of Frankie Boyle." Spiral Earth

"Revolutionary, elocutionary genius" ***** See Magazine

"The spoken word guru" Canadian Broadcasting Corporation

www.stevelarkin.com

Enjoy

Steve Larkin

Burning Eye

Supported using public funding by

ARTS COUNCIL ENGLAND

LOTTERY FUNDED

This edition published by Burning Eye Books 2019

www.burningeye.co.uk
@burningeyebooks

Burning Eye Books
15 West Hill, Portishead, BS20 6LG

ISBN ISBN 978-1-911570-65-3

Contents

Introduction

Welcome to my world!

I'm Steve Larkin. From being a teenager to the time of going to print with this book in my early forties, I have been focused on presenting my poetry and lyrics in a live environment as a 'performance poet'/'spoken word artist', and as a singer.

During the twenty-odd years that I've been doing this I have written a good number of pieces that have not found a home in the world of performance.

This book aims to bring all sides of my work together and to show sensitivity to the intended presentation of each piece. It also seeks to be sensitive to the way that different people engage with varying styles of literature through a variety of media.

My research has shown me that people rarely read a poetry collection from cover to cover; they mostly flick through them, and the average number of poems read in one sitting is 5.8!

In this collection, after each piece, you'll be presented with choices such as these to guide you to your next choice:

And to get around the whole square-peg-round-hole, oral/aural poetry in print, stage/page problem, you will, when it's appropriate, be given a QR code and a link like this:

stevelarkin.com/poemtit

These will take you to pages on my website that will house a number of multimedia treats in the form of film poems/animations, live video or audio footage of a performance, or a studio version of the poem/song in front of you. In fact, some of the pieces will only have a link and a picture and no printed text, because I feel that though they may have value in performance they don't work well enough on the page.

The symbols behind each title will tell you what audio/visual delight might be in store should you scan the code or follow the URL:

Video of a live
performance

Audio recording of a
live performance

Film poem or piece
of animation

Studio/radio
audio recording

Audio of
a song

Poem on
the page

With this book you have the option of getting your phone/computer out and seeing and hearing the particulars of my delivery, the nuance of tone and physicality, or you can hear the reaction of an audience laughing (in case you don't know where to laugh, like in a Shakespeare play!), or you can hear how lyrics have become part of a musical composition, or see how poetry has become part of film or public art, or you can have a simple technology-free silent read.

If this book is like the mean poetry collection, it'll spend most of its time next to a lavatory or a bed. This collection is probably the closest I will get to you without being in your bathroom or bed, and by the time you read this I may no longer be in a state of being, I may have become one of those financially successful dead poets, like Lord Byron, and your chances of seeing me live will be, like many who came into contact with Byron, buggered!

Oh, yes – this isn't suitable for children. Sorry! There are quite a few pieces that are, but vulnerable people should not be left unsupervised with this book.

So, thanks for taking a little time to meander through my mind.

Now, where to begin?

To help you get the most from your 5.8 poems I've designed a short questionnaire that will hopefully get you to the starting point that suits you best:

START HERE

Questionnaire

1. Do you:
a) get this idea of finding an appropriate starting point that might enhance the experience? *Go to 2*
b) just want to get straight to reading poems like you usually do in a poetry book? *Turn to page 90*

Questionnaire

2. I'D PREFER A PIECE TO:
a) be reasonably accessible with its meaning. *Go to 3*
b) take a lot of work to unpack its meaning. *Go to 4*

3. CHOOSE:
a) make me think. *Go to 5*
b) make me feel. *Go to 6*
c) make me laugh. *Go to 7*

4. WHICH IS MOST TRUE?
a) the author is dead, the reader's interpretation is paramount. *Turn to page 120*
b) clear intentions are important? *Go to 5*

5. CHOOSE:
a) political poetry. *Turn to page 22*
b) poetry politics. *Turn to page 16*
c) personal is political. *Turn to page 85*

6. WHICH OF THESE BEST DESCRIBES YOU?
a) I am more visually inspired than I am aurally inspired? *Turn to page 82*
b) I am more aurally inspired than I am visually inspired? *Go to 8.*

7. CAN SEXUAL SWEAR WORDS ADD EMPHASIS AND COMEDY VALUE?
a) no. *Turn to page 47*
b) fuck yeah! *Turn to page 117*

8. YOU'VE DECIDED TO LISTEN TO A BIT OF RADIO. IS IT GOING TO BE:
a) Radio 4 drama/feature or perhaps 5 live news? *Turn to page 108*
b) Radio 2 specialised music programme or perhaps 6 Music? *Go to 9.*

9. FANCY:

a) a poem/song? *Turn to page 64*
b) a song? *Turn to page 30*

Confused by talk of QR codes and links? *Turn to 'Roses' at the back of the book.*

.TV

TV was for Tuvalu
but is now for television.[*]
The media of internet
and TV merge.
The means of production
makes classic movie thieves.
The South Pacific spreads,
the sea swallows the island, people die,
as the online entry
makes a history revision:
TV was for Tuvalu
but is now for television.

---

*   I saw this phrase online. '.tv', like '.co.uk' or '.ca' for the UK and Canada respectively, is the website domain suffix that was used to denote websites registered in Tuvalu (the South Pacific island nation that it is thought will be the first to be completely submerged as sea levels rise as a consequence of climate change). It has now been coopted by those wanting to make websites appear like TV channels internationally.

The End of the World I P77
Sing-along-a climate change on your phone

One Big Sentence I P61
. . . about climate change

Giant I P68
Small poem about climate change.

Dead Poets' Soc.

'See me live before I die'
or 'See me *live* before I die'
is my new, new-media coded cry,
which, spoken,
doesn't work as a sight rhyme.

My new show's been conceived,
written, taken abroad,
performed on a bigger, brighter,
more open continent,
where I've been before.

It's been reviewed –
received rave reviews.
It's been
rehearsed,
rehearsed,
rehearsed,
and it's been very well advertised…
but ticket sales are low,
so low for the solo show,
no one seems to want to go – no!

The hope:
that the rush will far outweigh the advance.
Fat chance.
I'm staring at a massive bill for tax,
shivering – can't afford heat.
It's the wrong time of year
to sell tricks on the street –
I'd sell me a kidney
if I thought that they'd 'av' 'em,
but there seems no shortage of alkie cadavers.
This ain't rock and roll, or poetry of old –
no fat patronage, fine living and gout.
My funeral will be better attended,
no doubt.
(I hear they love a dead poet round here.
Yes, I hear they love a dead poet
round here.)

Because it seems gravitas only comes with the
    staid,
sentimental simplicity of Graves.
Poems only get spoken when a dyed
red paper poppy
gets adorned as a token,
in sombre tones,
when they've become tomes
dug from the tombs,
when the body gets dragged to glorify
and fetishise the dead,
and academics take the skeletal remains
and write *intertextuality*,
and *the poet's unspoken grappling*
with a suppressed sexuality.

Meanwhile up the road, close to boiling,
the blood pumps through the veins,
takes oxygen to the brain
of the living poet,
who breathes life and energy
into crafted poetic prose,
but nobody goes,
because the poet didn't have
the decency to die.
There's your problem, mate –
you're still alive!

Your mind controls your breathing,
you're making music with your speaking,
you're a highly strung but
finely tuned meat machine,
articulating/nuancing lyrical thinking.

If you want your words to carry on,
you've got to die, rot, become carrion,
let the vultures rip you up, deconstruct,
    decontextualise,
and shit you far and wide.

Yes, they love a dead poet round here:
ghostly echoey churches
and dimly lit lecture halls,
shadows on the walls,

resurrecting guarded cypher codes
in zombie tones.
Your sprightly voice isn't welcome here –
it's your own!
But they won't be told, because…
they love a dead poet round here.

True story:
Laurie Lee writes poetic prose.
It's genius, the audience suppose.
And when he sits an O-level exam
on work written by his own hand,
he scores a pathetic 43 per cent
and he's told
that he 'didn't understand the authorial intention'!
Perhaps they'll keep him in detention
until he's a better poet,
when he's dead, because…
they love a dead poet round here,
yes, they love a dead poet round here.
I'm thus surrounded by some
of the dullest dead writers round here,
and a cast of talented, frustrated,
living geniuses round here,

and I am depressed…
for I have spent
(what's looking increasingly likely to be)
a shorter-than-average lifetime creating oral poetry,
in an age where those that hold the keys
only seem to validate that that they can read.
The broadsheets, the literary elite and the mainstream
have never listened to a word I've said,
pop culture is now celebrity-driven drivel,
and my two favourite Beatles are dead!
And they like a dead artist round here,
they like to misrepresent minds around here,
they like to starve to death artists round here,
write 'the death of the author' round here,
throw their money at dead bards around here
whilst they charge them for living round here.
Make them pay through the nose
for the garret that they chose
in view of blue plaques around here.

And they're scared of an artist round here
who can speak their mind back without fear,
who can debunk the odd myth,
demystify art, tell them straight up
what the poem's about.
They fear those spoken soldiers
with no received pronunciation
who want to reload the canon
and with a bang make them listen.
They ignore or abhor
living poets they'd adore,
because they want a dead poet round here.

RIP Steve Larkin | P120
Steve Larkin is dead

The Only Truths I've Ever Known | P102
More spoken word manifesto.

The Post-Colonial Global Blues | P22
If you like a lyrical allusion or two.

The Midas Touch in Reverse

A ribald recounting of a disappointed life.

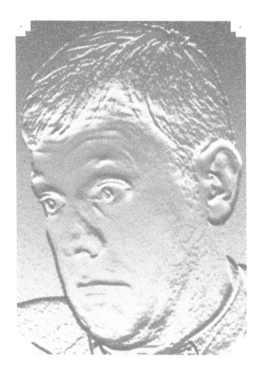

choose

Funny Old Game | P47
A lover of Socrates/Jimmy Greaves?
Football and philosophy like you've never seen

The Day I Fell in Love with a NatWest Service Point | P34
Capitalism – a love story

The Idiot's Guide to Writing an Idiot's Guide | P55
An author's vain attempt to be a commercial success.

Wannakah

A character from the wider world of spoken word – healing the world with the power of ego and the application of pithy anagrams.

STEVE LARKIN
.com/wan

CHOOSE

The Idiot's Guide to Writing an Idiot's Guide | P55
An author's vain attempt to be a commercial success.

The Meaning of Life | P42
More spoken word manifesto.

Incubator | P113
The world's most ambitious chat-up line:
Will you be an incubator for my DNA?

The Post-Colonial Global Blues

I've got those post-colonial global blues.
My shareholder's done left me,
followed loss leaders,
profit taken to a haven in the Cayman Isles.
And I'll be in negative equity;
if I act, I pay.
And I'm relocating to a town called *Jeopardy*,
where the headlines say there are *thousands of
    jobs* for me!
And a lifestyle choice of global homogeny,
and a concrete lack of unique identity.
I'm perpetually sent to post-war Coventry,
and I don't know what to do.
I've got those post-colonial global blues.

And I'll be crying tonight
as they're frying the shite
in the Amazon meat;
at least the kids'll be happy
with a fat-saturated treat,
but I am starved of oxygen,
going to ground like a fox again,
descending Brunel's human sewerage system,
a rat in the rat race,
drowning in the green wash from
'British' Petroleum.

The glass ceiling is mythical
is the message to the cynical,
but overshoot your station
and the barriers are physical.

Speculation won't help my present predicament,
trapped in a metropolis of tropical germs,
finding it very difficult to move.
I've got those post-colonial global blues.

And I'm stuck in a virtual queue,
and I know my call's not important to you;

a robot's done sent me to Timbuktu.
The accent cost just a penny or two.

Spare some copper if you don't mind.
What? From a Zambian pit that weren't even mine?!
Where they're stuffed in a hole in a debt-ridden mine?!
Metropole dictates: *Copper – I'll run power though mine.*

I could speak out freely through the telecom wires,
expose the situation to millions online,
but what exactly does protest do?
Police sit supping their Indian brew,
controlling the kettle for an hour or two.
So, junkie, on review:
I give you this metal that doesn't
belong to me or you to you,
you spike your vein, let the numbness flow through,
as the cash flows to an Afghan funding
suffering through opium roots,
I buy a poppy to support our troops,
one returns psychologically abused
and replaces you when you've turned blue.
I don't see what's in it for me or for you, or for the peasant farmers or
    for the troops;
we've all got those post-colonial global blues.

The colour supplement made it black and white,
divided the world with its polarised views,
London talking through north and south,
New York the other way round.

Can't stop people reproducin',
population'll soon be doublin' –
abortions in the basement
from mixing up the messages,
johnnies on the protestants
running all the governments.

Look out, kids,
it's original sin.

I don't know Zen,
but when you are born again
you'll be a duck or an alley cat
looking for a new trend.
The Nasdaq man selling futures to new men
wants several million dollar bills
but you've only got yen,
and from a spent to a vicious military force
this simply will not do;
you've got those
post-colonial global blues.

Get sick, stay sick,
pharmaceuticals get rich,
don't need a weatherman
to tell me that the world's fucked
and I need me a pick-me-up,
but I can't seem to see any English proper tea.
I'll have to resort to Colombian beans.
It'll Costa lotta Lotto tickets.
At least we'll see the profit trickle,
to Amazon – we won't see a nickel.
Triple-dip your grotty pickle,
it won't come back to you.
You've got those post-colonial global blues.

Staring at identical shops flogging sportswear,
from Leicester to Leicester Square,
that dedicated slaves to fashion.
I stand sweating, guilty, in my branded shoes.

I've got those post-colonial global blues.

At least *Blue Planet*'s on after the corporate news.

The world's getting bluer,
the seas are getting bigger,
the rich are getting fatter,
like a Christmas goose,
flying over continents
with an urge to consume,

and sometimes I wonder,
what am I gonna do?
cos there ain't no cure
for those post-colonial global blues.

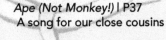

system malfunction

system malfunction
on the air conditioning unit
in the government building
which divides the city
with a spike
the central flash of light
from the downtrodden Leeds 9

system malfunction
bad operations device
is detected on error messages on
PCs in warm offices
the advice
taken with frustration
machine turn off and on again

system malfunction
on the ink jet printer settings
in the government building
which divides the grey sky
with a spike
the printed page administrates
and separates black from white

system malfunction
causing major congestion
faulty traffic lights at intersection
major arteries clogging
empty lives
fuelled by stress and necessity
get to work on time

and read the writing on the wall
cos the writing on the wall says
brain enslavement
brain enslavement
subservient automatons
supervise automation
as trust is put
in newfound
new labour

and time rich
and money poor
or time poor
and money rich
nobody's gonna
give you gifts
unless you sell your labour

forced a choice
conform to a life
tied to tidy office space
phone to ear
and screen to face
interface
with a ball and chain
living life
like a corporate slave
with the fear
of being made redundant
and all around
the signs flash
system malfunction

system malfunction
on the air conditioning unit
an engineer is paged to change a valve
attends the site for the sake of SLA
just another TLA
filters clogged need change
refers and goes away

system malfunction
on the fashion store lighting
in the clean city centre
junkies blocking consumer vision
moved away
coughing through fumes from
cars conceding right of way

system malfunction
on the air conditioning unit
atmosphere heats
vents circulate germs
for all to breathe

flustered staff crunch the
numbers and return to eat

system malfunction
input error on data program
mistake made by graduate
turned to drugs
somatised and comatosed
docile doped escaping
with intelligence numbed

read the writing on the wall
this is like *Nineteen Eighty-Four*

a meaningless expansion
of superfluous phones
and poverty wages
for workers and drones
angry defensive
hot bothered people
deny information and pass on calls
as we all become part of the Borg
an endless waste of human minds and time

read the writing on the wall
it appears to be ignored
by the countless corporate whores
polluting the air with
their new-style Model T Fords
crawling in at snail pace
to the pressurised useless office space
to do their meaningless daily chores
as governments tell us how good it is
implement insulting
minimum wage
and change the image of the modern slave
and masses continue
to live in a dirty world
where nothing works

system malfunction
goes undetected

heart disease goes unnoticed   heart disease goes unnoticed
lives lost to the office cars crashing
causing congestion
causing de
pression   causing agg
ression
all consume   people fume
error with human behaviour   error with
fuel injection
deaths for   greater

good
problem
                        engine
flood

death for greater good?

system malfunction
goes undetected
on the air conditioning unit
as the government building
burns to the ground
the ashes of a mindless civilisation
are washed away in a global flood
the human race is just energy displaced
as at last humanity finds its place
a short-lived parasite
a freak genetic mutation
a system malfunction

Original Sin

Steve Larkin song

Live in Vancouver – Canada

choose

system malfunction | P26
Bleak worldview challenge in small case extended metaphor. Don't expect to be any happier at the end – and it is the end, isn't it?

The London Eye | P51
More lyrical damnation of a rancid imperialist state.

Why Do I Still Live Here? | P106
In this grey imperialist state.

I Hate Poetry Please

Please request this poem to be read,
by an actor,
on Radio 4's *Poetry Please*.

Please let me hear a disconnected,
white middle-class accent,
with no vested interest
in poetic expression,
repeat the phrase
I hate Poetry Please!

Please appeal to (what I hope is)
the producer's hidden
sense of fun and mischief,
fear of social embarrassment,
and to her sense of duty to
perceived BBC balance, and
flood her inbox with a
request to hear a poem called
'I Hate Poetry Please'!

Please apply pressure on
yesterscouse token soft northern
comfort-voiced Waitrose salesman
Roger McGough, who, it seems, may
just have forgot the stuff that poetry's
made of: the essence of himself and his
visionary linguistic anarchic
oomph. Tell him thank you very much for
the *thank you very much*, for the Liverpool
scene and the Aintree Iron, the social zest
and lyrical philosophical depth, the
brilliant translation of the Molière text, so
ably presented in language steeped in access, but
please please please tell him:
I hate Poetry Please!

Because I love poems given
life by their maker,
with local knowledge
of her spoken arrangement,
because the poet thought of the way, not
just the what, of what's on the paper –

considered her birth, how she should be reared,
how we should feel her,
what she should be
if someone came to read her.

So please read this poem called
'I Hate Poetry Please'
out loud
on *Poetry Please*, please.
Shout,
Attention!
to the new modal army,
equipped with original poetic expression,
and *Stand easy, tropes; move away from the canon!*
to the boredom battalion,

trotting out tired, tedious, twee verses
from ever-decreasing circles
of poems whose endings don't leave us guessing
due to excessive repetition at
white bourgeois weddings:
well-trodden words from a handful of bards
who once trod the boards,
whilst stroking their beards,
with their poems about birds
or the supposed absurd,
which are now only exposed
in the classrooms of those
who bracket that faux-whimsical tone with
love, wisdom, and woe as
the inadequately narrow
definition they know
of a poem.

This is a cause of great depression.
There's a whole brave new world of poetic expression.

Now,
you could argue that *Poetry Please*
is doing no harm – let it be,
but I believe that *Poetry Please* restricts the
definition of what poetry can be and
suppresses the growth of the poetry scene.

If Radio 2 is the music station for
those that hate music,

then *Poetry Please* is the poetry programme for
those that hate muses.

No new inspiration, no genius,
nothing with unusual rhyme or meter.
No globetrotting antics, or
faraway fancies, not
much that ambles away from iambic.
No new themes.
Same old: *love, remembrance,
friendship, fellowship,*
recycled on calendars like seasonal worship,
parrot fashion repetition
devoid of passion like C of E hymns,
With endings that make you go *Hmm,*
not *Urgh!* or *Argh!* or *Jesus Christ!*
Because it's jumper-wearing, avoid all swearing, chicken in basket,
    don't stare at spastics* , biscuits are nice, don't like spice, meat
    and two vegetables, value your collectibles, keep it in the corner,
    de-value the performer, tune out, drawling, gnawing, boring poetry.
I want vibrant poems, preferably live, but at least from the living.

So read this poem
called 'I Hate Poetry Please'
on *Poetry Please,* please,
and please, please, please
change the nature of poetry, please.

Thanks,

Steve

----

*   I want to make it abundantly clear that I am embodying the voice of narrow
minded conservatives here, attempting to illuminate their inner thought-
processes and prejudices. I would never use that term myself, I believe it to
be a disablist slur.

Fat Sex | P39
Found piece from pile of women's magazines.

Wannakah | P21
Spoken word wankers

The Post-Colonial Global Blues | P22
With a bit of Dylan.

The Day I Fell in Love with a NatWest Service Point

With naïveté and innocence
I approached you one evening.
Your cute flashing words
caught my eye,
and you tempted me
with your charming request:
PLEASE INSERT YOUR CARD.
With such polite, delightful manner,
I could not resist.
I gave you my card as a token of my affection
    and said,
I love you,
my beautiful NatWest service point.

You asked me my name,
and I typed in my number.
I reckoned I was in.
I could tell by the tone of your
receptive bleeps.

And then you asked me,
CASH OR CASH WITH RECEIPT,
and I knew you loved me too!

Oh, how could it be,
my sweet NatWest service point?
They say love has no bounds,
but how could such a pristine beauty love such
    a fool,
and how could I love a machine?

So I pressed *CASH*, said,
To hell with the receipt;
let's live life on the edge!

But then you responded,
SORRY, YOU HAVE INSUFFICIENT FUNDS IN
    YOUR ACCOUNT…

and I knew it was over!

I should have realised.
Why should the figurehead
of part of a multinational, conglomerate, capitalist bank
love me:
a third-rate, third-year philosophy student,
on for a third at a third-rate polytechnic,
knowing briefly as I do
the processes that
brought about the Third Reich
and the Third World?
I've tried to tell them
that I will have money,
that I plan to be a famous poet,
a best-selling novelist,
and perhaps a filthy rich rock star
(depending on how it goes with my bass guitar).

But belief was never their strong point.
I'd try it on with the chick next door,
but I reckon she wouldn't listen,
and down the road I reckon she wouldn't say yes,
but I don't care;
if that so-and-so of a NatWest service point
values money more than me,
she can stick my card where the sun don't shine,
cos I'm gonna see
    if someone will buy me a pint.

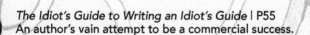
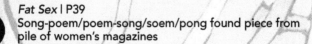
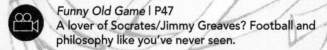

Kitten

A macabre story of a love affair that never happened.

Ape (Not Monkey!) | P37
Love fluffy animals?

I Met a Girl | P72
Inadvertent morality lessons that serial monogamists receive.

Striking Chords | P44
Me and my mandolin, who makes me sing.

Ape (Not Monkey!)
Steve Larkin song lyrics

I don't want to walk like you,
I don't want to talk like you,
I don't want to live with you,
imprisoned in a zoo.
A 'great ape' is what I am,
according to your school (of thought),
and when you boldly make this claim
you say that I'm like you (I'm not):

a fool like you.
I don't do as you do.
I don't take my hands, and make tools,
and then take those tools to the land.

I don't even walk like you,
and I don't even talk like you,
but if you watch your Disney film
then you'll believe I do.
But if you'll be so stupid, taking
truth from a cartoon,
then me and me friends,
we dance around,
sing *Scooby Dooby Doo*,

because we're fools for you,
you who can't see through
a perversion of the truth
where all I am is cute.

I hate to see projections of
your greedy evil eyes.
When you anthropomorphise,
that way danger lies.
You may say this song you hear
could not be made by apes;
a very limited consciousness
their spinal cord dictates...

so who produced this tune?
Not me, the orangutan, that's true.
It's from a man in an ape suit,
with a message just for you,

which is:

you must learn the dismal fact
that I am going to die,
and you must be enlightened
by the frightening reason why.
The reason that my genotype
is going to be no more
is because the *Homo sapiens*
have wiped the forest floor

for their food and their fuel.
Now I don't know what to do,
because the human being is being cruel.

So, last call for the orange man of the forest,
last call for the ancient man of the trees.

Last call for the orange man of the forest,
last time he'll call out his territory.

Last call for the orange man of the forest,
or last nail in the coffin of our ancestry.

I don't want to walk like you,
I don't want to talk like you,
I don't want to live with you, imprisoned in a zoo.

I want to live my life in trees,
eating different fruits.
I want this beautiful life I see
to always continue.
Do you?

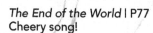

Can We Be Friends? | P83
Low-definition song writing

The End of the World | P77
Cheery song!

A Contrived Poem... | P117
Have a Merry Christmas... with B&Q!

Fat Sex

This contains many actual quotes (in italics) from a single pile of young women's magazines I found in an ex-girlfriend's bathroom.

Every woman's magazine,
every front cover,
takes its theme
from the woman's dream
to be a better lover.

And every woman's magazine –
New Woman, Best,
Vogue, Zest –
completely obsessed
with achieving better sex.

Every woman's magazine
blazoned across their fronts
words that stir insecurity
'bout the size of hips
and tits and bums.

Every woman's magazine
sells its ideals,
aggressively asserts
the feared fact
that she is *too fat.*

In every woman's magazine
two words will stand out,
words with which girls
become obsessed –
the words *fat* and *sex*

Fat and *sex.*
Fat and *sex.*
Completely obsessed
with *fat* and *sex.*
It's the *fat sex,* the *fat sex,*
the *fat sex* appeal.

Every woman's magazine

tells females that read it
to *have your cake and eat it.*
Half the calories, twice the size,
Get your regular exercise
for *great boobs and tight bums.*
Here comes another one –
another man in your thighs,
great sex with no ties.

Yes, every woman's magazine,
completely obsessed with *fat* and *sex.*

It's the *fat sex,* the *fat sex,*
the fat sex appeal.

And *more sex!*
And *best sex!*

Because this…
This is *New Woman.*
The monsters the magazines created.

Every New Woman
is *saggy, wrinkly, blotchy.*
Every New Woman
needs *the guide to perfect skin.*
Every New Woman
needs *great boobs and tight bums,*
the secret of an easy orgasm –
needs flesh,
obsessed with flesh.

With *make-up kits and fashion tips,*
health and beauty dieting,
blokes and cooking,

boils down to *fat* and *sex.*
Better sex this Saturday,
look like a babe when you feel like a blob,
dump the diet, drop the pounds.
Are there any men around?

For *fat sex,* the *fat sex,*
the *fat sex* appeal.

And *good sex,*
and *better sex,*
and *more sex,*
more sex,
more sex!

Oh Oh Oh – Oh-gasmic.
She knows:
The scientific guide to coming like a train!
The scientific guide to coming like a train!!
Again and again and again and again!!!

Every woman's magazine
craves commercial success,
and caters for the craving
of woman and her sex.

And every woman's magazine
creates that craving,
and I just think it's time that they stopped misbehaving.
If women get obsessed completely with sex,
men already are,
so then there's nothing left.

Kitten | P36
A true story of a love affair that never happened.

The Idiot's Guide to Writing an Idiot's Guide | P55
An author's vain attempt to be a commercial success.

Woman's Hour Second Breakfast | P54
Further extension of the body of work on the body.

The Meaning of Life

The Meaning of Life –
it's a one-hour lecture
with two hours after
for questions and answers.

The form is quite simple:
I'll state my case,
develop my argument
and back it up with quotes
from the masters.

The Meaning of Life –
it's a one-hour lecture.
When I make a joke…
I'll pause for your laughter.

Feel free to make notes.
I've a list of the quotes
to include in your essay,
due next semester.

The Meaning of Life –
it's a one-hour lecture.
You won't understand,
but then you don't have to.

The essay is due March 25;
the title, you know,
is *The Meaning of Life*,
course code PHI 209.

The Meaning of Life –
it's a one-hour lecture.
You'll gain nothing new,
but then you don't have to;
just make good notes
and write them out neatly,
apply to the essay,
plagiarise discreetly.

The Meaning of Life –
it's a one-hour lecture

and the title of my new book,
published by Macmillan,
priced £19.99.
It's a course text,
and its purchase is mandatory.
I repeat, its purchase is mandatory.

The Meaning of Life –
it's quite simple, really.
To me, anyway, the meaning of life is making hard cash from the
modern-day scam we've come to call education.

Any questions?

Yes – that's *The Meaning of Life – Modern-Day Approaches to
Philosophical Questions*, available at the university bookshop, priced
£19.99.

Can We Be Friends? | P83
Low-definition song writing

Live in Leeds | P58
'Common People' for the twenty-first century in
ranting form.

Dead Poets' Soc. | P16
Spoken word whinging!

Striking Chords

I sing to my mandolin,
tell her of other lovers
with equally glorious contours,
delicious curves and slender bodies
with smooth and shining surfaces.
I tell her of those real and imagined:
the girl from next door or the foreign shore,
the fallen angel,
the cleaner with the film star looks,
the filthy actress,
the porcelain doll in the country house,
the aggressive nymphomaniac imp.
I tell her of all the steamy affairs
all over the world,
from idyllic meadows
to the cargo bays of ships.
I tell her of love and loss and confusion.
I tell her of addiction to good times and beauty.
I cry on her mahogany,
evoke the rainforest memory,
the pouring down
of my past
on this dead wood.
My emotional sponge.

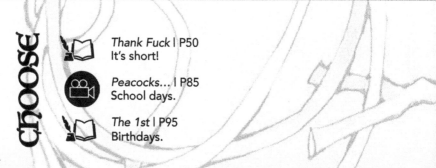

choose

Thank Fuck I P50
It's short!

Peacocks... I P85
School days.

The 1st I P95
Birthdays.

Curtains

The purchasing of curtains
is the death of your sex life.
What do you think those newlyweds do
when they lock themselves inside?
They focus thoughts on furniture
and interior design,
on ways to keep their new safe haven,
ways to build divides.
A sanctuary from overexposure from their
primitive hunting times:
those drunken idiots at parties,
dancing badly through the night,
the aggressive competitive workers
with their eyes set on the prize
of accumulating promotions
and accruing husbands and wives.
And when that shit's done and dusted,
the deposit on the nest,
she'll sit on the eggs,
find new ways to avoid his wanting gaze
like talking at length about tasteful drapes
of elegant material and afternoon shade.
Not the gory velvet from their clubbing days,
but the virginal white
evocative of her wedding veil.
His interest feigned,
he'll plan his escape
and make a new bed
for planting excess seeds in his potting shed.

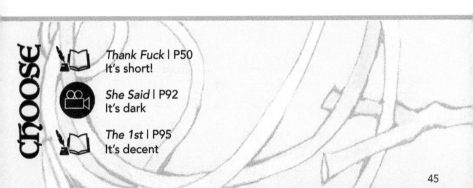

choose

Thank Fuck | P50
It's short!

She Said | P92
It's dark

The 1st | P95
It's decent

The Liberal Property Owner

Inflatable Buddha song

He's a liberal property owner,
building up a nest egg for
when he gets older.

He's quiet a nice guy,
he's giving it a try.
He's trying his best
to live an ethical life,
but...

PRIVATE PROPERTY KEEP OUT
TRESPASSERS WILL BE PROSECUTED TO THE FULL EXTENT OF THE LAW

CHOOSE

Oi, Codger | P99
Commissioned piece that aims to encourage older people to take up exercise.

Slowly, Slowly, Cowley Road | P82
Where all the good people live and pay extortionate rent.

She Said | P92
Her voice needs to be heard, I'd say.

Funny Old Game

University was a bit tricky for me,
being a football fan
doing a philosophy degree.

It meant I had a diverse circle of friends
from different ends
of the spectrum of beliefs.

On one side there was Hugh,
an epistemological rationalist thinker
who toyed with the idea of solipsism,
and then there was Dave…
a Newcastle United fan.

The pub was never fun
when we all went out.
A few pints of lager,
a chat about life.
Lively discussions were… difficult.

On one side Hugh is telling me,
Augustine's argument is fundamentally flawed
and, although logically true,
I'd rather take Kierkegaard's view,
because any belief in a transcendental being is
essentially an irrational belief; however, the existence
of a god is the crux for all western philosophy.
And Dave says,
There's definitely a god,
you've just gotta believe in him.
There's definitely a god
and his name is Kevin Keegan.

Though since he left United,
I think I'd agree with Nietzsche
that God is dead.

It was difficult to have conversations
that they both understood
without Hugh becoming patronising,
or Dave just taking the piss.

I'd be having two conversations simultaneously,
assessing the results from Saturday
whilst pontificating and picking at Plato.

Dave occasionally picked on Hugh:
You're all the same, you soft Southern intellectual types

ALL GENERALISATIONS ARE DANGEROUS – EVEN THIS ONE.
THAT'S A QUOTE FROM EMERSON.

Emerson? Dave says.
He's doing quite well at Deportivo La Coruña
but I never really rated him at 'Boro.

It was hard to get Hugh and Dave to speak, let alone agree,
but they both really rated Socrates,
one for his teaching of Plato
and one for that overhead kick against Mexico.

One day Hugh was asking me about the influence of the Continentals
        on the modern-day school of thought
when Dave butts in:
Well, they've got a lot of skill, like, them continentals,
but I can't abide all that divin'.

I remember the day when it all changed,
the day that Dave
told us about some French-Algerian philosopher,
he couldn't remember his name,
Dave told us that this guy was also a professional goalkeeper,
and that this guy claimed that
in his ten years between the posts
he learned more about life
than he did in a lifetime
pondering the meaning of life.

He said we should stop asking questions
that can never be answered,
find a team to support and
start reading the sports sections
of newspapers rather than philosophical journals.

So we did.

I still support Leeds,
and Hugh, quite predictably,
coming from Middlesex,
supports Manchester United.

And Dave?
    Dave now lectures at Newcastle University on the influence of
    deconstructionism on modern-day football management.

It's a funny old game – philosophy.

Can We Be Friends? | P83
Low-definition song writing

Live in Leeds | P58
'Common People' for the twenty-first century in
ranting form.

Dead Poets' Soc. | P16
Spoken word whinging!

Thank Fuck

I'd been careful not to tell her
that I loved her in a fit of passion,
but it happened.
Not the usual laddish
Howay the lads! with the injection
of the army of my selfish gene.
But *I love you, do you love me?*
No, she said, *but you're a grand fuck,*
and cackled with the same empirical attitude
that we'd conditioned ourselves to respect,
but not love.
Thank fuck.

Curtains I P45
Love and marriage go together like poetry and cynicism

We Are the Boys for Fun and Noise I P96
A Larkin poem

Original Sin I P30
My first song

The London Eye

Welcome to the London Eye,
I'm gonna take you on a ride.
Welcome to the London Eye,
I'm gonna take you deep inside.

There are points of interest,
things to see,
and a hotchpotch version of history.
There's a history of treachery
in a constitutional monarchy,
a constitutional monarchy
that poses as democracy.
I'll show you things you'll never see,
you'll never see on a TV screen.

On the right you'll see the sight
of England's proud financial might.
On the left look up the Thames;
it's a stinking grey polluted mess.
Up ahead beyond Big Ben:
Victoria and Waterloo –
station names reminding you
of monarchy and victory,
and an economy that's serving you,
held together with the use of guns.

Welcome to the London Eye,
a corporate logo in disguise.
Welcome to the London Eye,
I'm gonna take you for a ride.

There are points of retail,
things to buy
for those that value chintz and treats.
There's a particular habit of gluttony
in a *laissez-faire* economy
and institutional poverty
that poses as demography,
to secure the trade and guarantee
the growth of a baseless economy.

Moored for good on the eastern bank,

51

there sits *Belfast* like a tank,
opposite the western bank,
where the gold standard sadly sank.
In its place endorsed state,
dictating tax and interest rates,
cancerous growth of capital venture,
the world's resources out to tender,
controlled by an elite of technocrats
backed up by supposed democrats.

Welcome to the London Eye,
a hundred metres in the sky.
Welcome to the London Eye,
a thirty-minute waste of time.

There are points of interest,
things to see,
and a hotchpotch version of history.
There's a history of treachery
in a constitutional monarchy,
a constitutional monarchy
that poses as democracy.
I'll show you things you'll never see,
you'll never see on the BBC.

On the right, past London Bridge,
you'll see what past colonials built.
In the air to the east and west
it's a stinking grey polluted mess.
Up ahead, past parliament,
Westminster Abbey rears its head.
Hidden between and set in stone,
Oliver Cromwell sets the tone
for Church of England xenophobes to
rule the earth with the excuse of Christ.

Welcome to the London Eye,
lighting up the London sky.
Welcome to the London Eye,
a thing to do before you die.

See London – the capital city of the UK,
the fifty-first state of the USA.
Well, I hope you have a very nice day!

Because as the wheel raises your fat, gullible,
American tourist arse up into the London sky,
spins you round,
and gently places it back down,

I'll be dreaming
of razing London
to the ground.

choose

Giant | P68
Small poem about climate change

Live in Leeds | P58
'Common People' for the twenty-first century in
ranting form

Sonny – Prestatyn | P105
A Philip Larkin poem rebooted

Woman's Hour Second Breakfast

Just what happens in the uterus of the
obese woman to make her child so fat?
The stand-in Radio 4 presenter's tone
comically flat.
I laugh.
Outside on the pavement,
waddling past, a young mother,
a ball of blubber and pram,
is the last to return from the school 'run';
her imposing profile and then surprise
sideways glance take me aback.
I reduce my focus,
zoom out to my window reflection,
where I notice that I'm starting to look like my dad!
I think of the way his face contorts,
nose crumpled, if he has to utter the word *fat*.
Just what happened to him at school?
Was he bullied for being too thin?
I tune back in.
An expert is talking of *preconceptual care*.
I tune back out
and butter my toast.

Fat Sex | P39
Body fascists

She Said | P92
Her voice needs to be heard, I'd say

Oi, Codger! | P99
The keep-fit poem for wrinklies!

The Idiot's Guide to Writing an Idiot's Guide

Find a niche subject, one that no one's written
    about before.
Get some experience in the field, enough to get
    your foot in the door.
Condense the main activities of the subject to a
    one-page list.
Voilà! You have your contents page.
Now write an extensive bibliography
of related titles that you never actually read,
    except for, well, the titles,
contents, first page, indices, and anything in
    bold that might have looked vital.
Now that's the majority of the book written. Well
    done!
Time to make this sandwich,
with a tedious repetitive writing style that you
    can fill the book with.

Now this middle section, or the 'content', is far
    less important;
the chances of anyone getting this far are more
    slender than, well… the content.
So employ your tedious repetitive writing style
    ad infinitum,
ensuring that you take great care to over-explain
    every single item,
and ensure you refer back constantly to
    everything that you've already written.
Chances are, if it's obvious,
that it'll neatly fit in
with your tedious repetitive writing style
on the subject matter
on which you are claiming some 'expertise' with
    reminders in each chapter
of your experience in the field
which will justify the purchase
to anyone who might have bought it.

To further validate your repeated
I am an expert in this field, honest! chorus,
use a thesaurus…

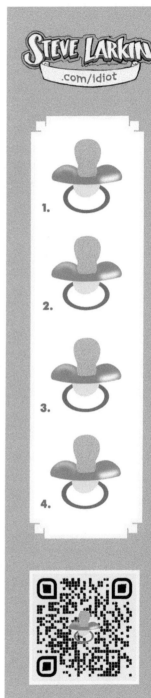

Look to find a source for greater vocabulary!

Try to extend your lexicon!

Attempt to increase the wordlist that you utilise!

Remember your idiot reader is the type of person who will let a text wash over them rather than scrutinise or analyse.

Give them something to help visualise.
Drop in an illustrated quote from a famous Greek thinker like
     Euripides or Aristotle,
one which adds some gravitas to what is essentially inane filler
     twaddle.

This is an idiot's guide, so remember to:
repeat,
repeat,
repeat.
The language should be simple.
The sentences short.

And remember this is an idiot's guide, so:
repeat,
repeat,
repeat.

Do: Include a dos and don'ts list.

Don't: Have too much narrative text that isn't separated.

Do: Separate large blocks of text.

Don't: Not have a dos and don'ts list.

Do: Repeat the dos and don'ts list with a summary.

Don't: Not repeat the dos and don'ts with a summary.

The dos and don'ts list should then be summarised with a small piece of narrative text.

Once again, the sentences should be short.

The midsection of each chapter should employ language that is full of vacuous diction, words and phrases that can be seen on the page but don't really register in the brain; sentences that are so long, that have so many clauses (the majority completely unnecessary) that they fill up the chapters nicely, because, remember, you are writing for idiots with only a passing interest in the subject, so these sentences should only come in the middle of paragraphs, where the reader won't notice that they are excessively long; this way it'll appear to the reader that they are being presented with a lot of information, getting value for money, and reading a text that has had a lot of effort put into making it comprehensive.

Final sentences can be short.

- Split up the text with bullet points
- Take up a lot of space on the page with bullet points
- Fill up the book with bullet points

At the end of every chapter say exactly the same thing in a summary section, in a different font, so that the reader knows at a glance that a summary is happening.

Include a dos and don'ts summary using bullet points.

Remember this is an idiot's guide, so repeat, repeat, repeat,

repeat, repeat, repeat,
repeat, repeat, repeat,
repeat, repeat, repeat,
repeat, repeat, repeat,
repeat, repeat, repeat,
repeat, repeat, repeat.

In conclusion, if you have little or no imagination, have barely a trace of integrity, care not for artistry, are motivated solely by the making of money, then why not waste your life, the small amount of writing skill that you possess, the world's natural resources, and your gullible readers' time by penning the perfect idiot's guide?

Sonny – Prestatyn | P105
A Philip Larkin poem rebooted

Live in Leeds | P58
'Common People' for the twenty-first century in ranting form.

Wannakah | P21
A character from the wider wankier world of spoken word

Live in Leeds

Live in Leeds,
live in Leeds,
live in any northern university city,
live in Manchester, Liverpool, or Sheffield.

Live in Leeds,
live in Leeds,
live in a run-down terrace
in Hyde Park or Headingley,

anywhere that's a far cry
from the neat streets
that are a treat for the *nouveau riche*.

Live in Leeds cos it's wicked.
Live in Leeds cos it's cool.
Spend your time taking drugs and talking about
    clubs,
because there's fuck all else to do.

Live in Leeds,
live in Leeds,
live in Leeds,
please!

Live in Leeds,
live in Leeds,
live in any northern university city,
live in Newcastle, Nottingham, or Hull.

Live in Leeds,
live in Leeds,
take on the student ethos of right on beliefs,
the ones that you keep out of the reach
of those with clothes
too cheap to join your clique.

Live in Leeds cos it's *sorted*.
Live in Leeds cos it's *safe*.
Get some cash from your dad,
grow some mould in your bath,
and sleep throughout your days.

Live in Leeds,
live in Leeds,
live in Leeds,
please!

Be my guest,

but when you've left,
just be careful what you represent.
If you go travelling round Africa or Asia,
don't go spouting details of inner-city race and hate
that you gained watching telly in leafy suburbia.

If people ask about living in Yorkshire,
don't paint Leeds as some glorious utopia
when all you saw was student flats,
student clubs, and cheap deals on beer.

If you spend three years considering
left-wing or liberal beliefs,
don't leave, and leave them behind,
just to rejoin your own kind:
the mercenary greedy uncaring right.

And if people stop you in the street
asking you to join Amnesty or Greenpeace – join!
Don't just wear the badges like some plastic fantastic hippie who
     can't help but say *yippee* at the prospect of becoming the latest
     McTit to eat the latest McShit,
like vegetarians who preach but still eat meat –
I know them; I've had sexually fulfilling but emotionally frustrating
     relationships with *New Woman* – supposed neo-feminists who
     harp on about rights when all they want is wealth for the sake of
     their pride, a man with a fat wallet and a fast car and something
     to fuel their fat ego; well, if that's you, then go, and leave the rest
     to live in Leeds.

Live in Leeds,
live in Leeds,
enjoy your time,
have fun with the people that you meet.

Live in Leeds,
live in Leeds,

spend a student loan on a holiday in Crete;
if I could, I would!

Live in Leeds,
live in Leeds,
climb to the top of the social and intellectual tree,
then leave.

But just remember that you're just passing through,
like changing trains at Crewe.
Yeah, use your brain and think,
but don't think that because you take fashionable drugs and walk
    around half-cut that you're a cut above the rest, the uneducated
    masses of oppressed,
because you consider yourself part of an ethical elite
but you're still clueless peasants as far as I can see

Live in Trees I P110
'Live in Leeds' from the perspective of a former
angry young man still clinging to utopian ideals

One Big Sentence I P61
Bring back hanging!

Funny Old Game I P47
Football and philosophy fun.

One Big Sentence

I believe in the right to life and find it hard to see how quite so many feel so free to dole out death as a punishment for crimes; mind, I can see nothing but defence for the utilitarian ideal of the greatest good for the greatest number, perhaps the best of what is left when you take away the extreme and unreasonable ideologies from the right and the left, and if there is such a thing as society then society should work together to eliminate crimes for the benefit of humankind by effecting a deterrent that has the greatest impact on what we can agree is bad, which means that as a society we can take into consideration the right to life but ultimately we should make the assumption that the greatest good for the greatest number is the one guiding principle that we should take to make the laws that ultimately dictate the way we live our lives, because life is for living, and if we believe in the right to life then we should work out a way of giving the right to life to the greatest number of people that we can give it to, because if a single death saves a million lives then surely we cannot deny that that one guy who takes a million lives does not have a million times the right to life of the million that will die as a consequence of his actions: actions that spell complete disaster for not just the victims of such crimes but also the victims' wives, husbands, mothers, brothers, friends and lovers, whose lives like a bubble will burst, and so it is the worst of crimes that should be the first of crimes to eliminate from our world, and so first we must define crime, and to save time let us define crime as an action taken against the law – a law set by a social norm – committed with malice aforethought, and it is this malice aforethought that is, of course, the cause of all the crime that we want to prevent with the selection of a deterrent, and to have malice afore-thought you must have prior knowledge of the odious consequences that you can cause, and the most catastrophic odious consequence that you can cause is multiple deaths; the biggest threat of multiple deaths (according to informed scientists, who we will just have to trust know the best) is the magnitude and range of disasters that will occur with climate change, and climate change is the effect of the release of CO_2 into the atmosphere; releasing CO_2 into the atmosphere is the effect of burning fossil fuels; we all know that burning fossil fuels releases CO_2, which causes climate change, and that climate change causes death, so to burn fossil fuels is to act with malice aforethought to commit murder – mass murder – and because I believe in the right to life for the millions who will die if sea levels rise, because I care about potential death in places like Holland, Cumbria and Bangladesh, and because I believe that the conceivable catastrophe that could be caused by climate change is something that we can prevent, then I believe that we should bring back hanging for bicycle theft; yes, bring back hanging for bicycle theft, because I believe in the right to life but ultimately make the assumption that the greatest good for the greatest number is the one guiding principle that we should take to make the laws that ultimately dictate the way we live our lives, and if we can make an example of the enemies of the prevention of climate change with a careful and choice selection of an effective deterrent instead of crude trade in death for death – an eye for an eye – then we will look to find a crime committed against the most vulnerable and helpful people, the people who sustain human life by taking part in the race on a bike, the people who deny themselves the pleasure of speed and the greed of convenient consumption, the people with the gall and gumption to go against the grain because they believe that they can gain the right to life for future generations, and you may say with some justification that this unusual approach is letting off killers scot-free, but that need not be if we see that we implement the laws to hit them where it hurts, which we can do if we outlaw oil, condemn coal, make sustainable life the one uniting goal, enforce the law, fine the rich power-producing pirates, imprison the oh-so-freely polluting pilots and drivers, but let's not dole out death willy-nilly, because I believe in the right to life, and I believe that the right to life is something that we should respect and protect, except we should bring back hanging for bicycle theft.

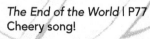

Hooligans

Waving your Union Jack banners
about the place,
so full of nationalist pride
you forget the people
that died to create
this obnoxious pompous state.
Screeching and shouting
at the top of your ugly voices
to the bland old sounds
of the patriotic chants.
Massed together like a pack of dogs.
United together – United Kingdom thugs.
Hooligans, you're all hooligans.
Of country and colour you boast,
the most selfish nation you toast.
Angrily and stubbornly,
ignorant right-wing bully boys
who never stop to think
how we coloured the globe in pink.
Your forefathers trashed Aborigines' skulls,
made slaves of Africans formerly free,
and dropped countless pointless bombs,
and still you scream your smug songs…
Well, as you can guess, I've never liked
Last Night at the Proms.

Electoral Poetry Commission | P79
Political piece for BBC radio

The London Eye | P51
The epicentre of colonial evil

Black Friday | P108
Way too early on BBC Breakfast

Melody

1.
Face to face,
on a high street,
on a sunny afternoon.
We shone our eyes
at one another,
blinking in disbelief,
making strobe-like patterns
from the flashes
of two ironic points of light
in spite of passing masses.
Dizzied
with a sweet sense
of loving success.
Filling myself with
her sweet scent.
The tall sun heated our necks,
and I was flooded with a passion
as consumers trudged by
with their empty bags of fashion.

She stood head and shoulders
above the rest,
and I guessed she
was the one to rescue me
from a fate worse than death.
And this was the moment we met.
I recall the moment
clearly in my memory,
fixed to the eyes
of a girl called Melody,
on top of the hill
in a city prone to flooding,
trying to get her money
through charity mugging.
She was much taller than me
and she made me look up,

her dark beauty in stark contrast
to the midday sun.

64

I'd decided that I wanted to do good,
and I thought she probably should,
and I thought that I might just fall in love,
and I thought that she possibly would.

Melody studies ancient history
here at the university,
connected to subsequently
rejected philosophy.

Is Melody the one for me?
We'll wait and see.

2.
Side to side,
at a party,
on a muggy stormy night.
I was dragged
to the floor to chat
to dour people
dressed in black.
She perched above the rest
in a pastel-coloured dress,
and I was
dazzled
with an irrational fear
of loving failure,
filling myself with
stress and pressure.
The intensity of humidity
added to my growing frustration.
My eyes tried to distract,
to attract talk of
conservation, but
she sat ignoring
my obvious request,
and I guessed she
was not the one to rescue me
from a fate worse than death,
and I thought back to the moment
we met.
I try to recall the moment –
it's fading in my memory.
I'm looking to the eyes

of a girl called Melody,
halfway up a hill
in a city prone to flooding,
trying to get her money
to do some good with.
She was much taller than me.
I had to stretch to her face,
which was fading away
in the afternoon shade.
Still sure that I wanted to do
good,
and sure that she definitely
should,
but not sure that I wanted to fall in love,
and not sure if she possibly
would.

Melody studies ancient history
here at the university,
connected to subsequently
rejected philosophy.

Is Melody the one for me?
We'll wait and see.

3.
Back to back,
on a tube train,
the day of a solar eclipse.
We narrowed eyes at one another,
recalling our reflections
in the strobe-like patterns
made by flashes
of demonic electric light
amidst consumer masses.
Puzzled, with a dim sense
of recognition.
Filling myself with scent and poison,
the automatic stairs thrust us to a dark end.
We reacquainted there and then;
as consumers pointed to the dark sun
again we bucked the trend as she laid
against a railing,
to explain how she

was chained to
consumer debt,
and I tried to recall the moment we met.
I can't recall the moment
clearly in memory,
looking for the eyes of a girl called Melody
at the base of the hill as the city starts to flood,
wading through the water, the silt and mud.
She was much stronger than me and I reached for her hand,
to take me away and to reach dry land,
but she refused to do anything good,
as I was sure she probably would.
I didn't think about falling in love.
I'm not sure if she even could.

No, Melody is not the one for me.
Melody studies ancient history,
Melody studies ancient history,
and Melody *is* ancient history.

The End of the World | P77
Cheery song!

Incubator | P113
The world's most ambitious chat-up line: Will you
be an incubator for my DNA?

Lemming Me Wrong | P69
Another woman's climate change story?

Giant

Never trust people who want that sort of power!
emerged echoing from the giant cooling tower.
Operations down.
Blackout – dim-witted thinking – *kettle!*
No lightbulb moment,
just brutal movement.
The grey modern-day monoliths run out of steam,
the energy giant brought to its knees,
albeit temporarily,
because in the darkness
the black uniforms and boots beat back the path
of least resistance.
The road to the coal is open.

Never trust people who want that sort of power.

Wash More | P74
Those smelly little people who fight the giants

Hooligans | P63
Land of hope and glory!

Electoral Poetry Commission 2015 | P79
Political piece for BBC radio

Lemming Me Wrong

Eyes prised from TV's perpetual surprise,
I gaze lazily at the world map,
focus on Lake Chad.

The documentary is showing me
global warming, drought, energy,
famine, poverty, dust.
No sense or evidence of any mystical
saviour conducting acts of love.

Electrons power round a circuit,
orange heat glows around my feet,
the energy burns,
I warm and ignore
the splash, the bang, and the scream
from next door.

The canine barks,
frantically sniffs
the back of the telly
for the scent of the bitch
it spotted running,
hunting quality dog food.
Fooled by the human's machine,
sniffing the aerial cable,
unable to contemplate
the shallow image
on the silver screen,
the dog, perplexed,
chews on a rubber bone.

As father screams to
son to get on the phone,
the bath water bubbles like a Jacuzzi,
my kettle's steam
hits the ceiling, click!
Connect:
vapour hits the tropopause over scorching equator;
Chadians, the poorest nation of Africans,
span the scorched GDP-weak land

and Lake Chad,
the blue with the thin strip of green
on the yellow bit of the map.

Scientists receive message on machine,
pack instruments, don glasses,
journey through tunnels
to tower block,
take elevator,
walk down corridor,
knock five times on door.

Shown to the bathroom
by emotional husband,
their examination evoked
a vocal response
when the husband sobbed,
What went through her head?
Electricity, they both said.

Thirty floors of central heating,
poorly insulated, empty lives,
the scientist and the dog
keep warm and ignore
the problems that they saw.

The plaster on the cracks is crumbling.
Immediate safety procs the done thing,
the trip switch, the power cut
to my consumptive cathode ray,
the darkness.
Next door the woman is rigid in the bathtub
teeth ground tightly together
on the charred remains of her dumb tongue,
the entrance to the universe bonded shut,
circuit completed, arms hugging television,
holding it tightly to her bust;
as the desert extends on the moonlit land,
another one bites the dust.
And I am thrust into the darkness,
with access to evidence – the map.

So I accept that I must speak up,
and I will,
or I will forever hold my tongue,
like this giving mother has done.

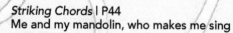

Striking Chords | P44
Me and my mandolin, who makes me sing

Original Sin | P30
My first song

Electoral Poetry Commission 2015 | P79
Political piece for BBC radio

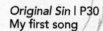

I Met a Girl

Inflatable Buddha song

At time of going to print, the only recording of this was a live one produced by self-acclaimed 'creative fucking genius' Martin Rushent – legendary producer of the Stranglers/Human League et al. The lyrics come thick and fast with a lot of reverb. People who've read them appreciate that the piece is a youthful, probably misguided, attempt at celebrating the inadvertent positive influence that the subjects had on a serial monogamist, and that it isn't, as a casual listener might infer, about bragging about sexual conquests. One for the website if you fancy a quick-fire singalong challenge!

 *Love Is War* | P73
Looks like we can't be friends

 Melody | P64
A pan-dimensional apocalyptic love poem

 The Midas Touch in Reverse | P20
I'm cursed!

Love Is War

Spoken word with music –
'Man Fights Machine and Looses'
by Uncool Sam
Written in an 'angry young man'
stage with electronica band Valley Forge.

Wash More

I respect the fact that
you've taken a different path
from the *Untermensch.*

I quite like the fact
that you can allude to Nietzsche
in a well-constructed sentence.

I'm cock-a-hoop that from these philosophical roots
you've built beliefs
that, like the junk that you
pick up from the streets,
you firmly intend to reuse.

I'm chuffed to bits you've made a table out of a
    disused door.
I love the way you smack
capitalism firmly in the jaw.

Why, you're like a more
radical version of Al Gore!
I adore the fact that you're so fiercely, nay, violently
    anti-war!

I just wish you'd wash more.
Yes, I just wish you'd wash more.

Does your squat not
have running water?
Not sure how I feel about
you sponging resources,
but the smell tells me the
private company ought to
supply you for free as a
simple act of benevolence to
the local bill-paying community,
as part of their
corporate social responsibility.

I share your views on the need for a
techno-global proletariat movement.
For the disenfranchised to

get connected to the net,
use the means of production
in an act of self-government.
Why, it's what Marx and Engels intended.
Let me join in – just move my computer
to a room with a vent in.

I intend to think globally and act locally
when the fumes from your arse
have stopped choking me.

Because when you speak –
people listen.
You give them a choice.
Because your breath smells like a
rat crawled up your arse and died,
and you shat it and ate it,
in a pathetic attempt
to end waste and famine.
So the choice you give is this:
hold your nose, or vomit.

Yes, I just wish you'd wash more.
It seems that the clothes that you sweat in when you mosh wore,
the damp fibres rubbing bacteria into newly made spot pores.
Please stop dancing; could this rancid smell possibly waft more?
What do you think a cloth's for?
Your house smells like the band's wardrobe on the bus of a goths'
    tour,
your pants are older than the Nordic god Thor.
I don't want you to give up
and join the rat race once more;

I wish you well in your endeavour
to start a peaceful war.
In your ideology, just like your bedroom,
I see no flaw(/floor).
I just wish you'd wash more.

I *want* you to turn on, tune in and drop out,
just don't want you to drop in unannounced
before I have the chance to get the fumigating chemicals out.

Now, I love your commitment to political change,

to the overthrowing of the new world order,
even if it's informed by a personality disorder.

I respect your belief in sentient beings,
the compassion shown to bacterial disease.
Fight the good fight, my friend –
make the world take notice.
Maybe before that public meeting, though,
you could sort out your halitosis.

Cos I'm rooting for the underdog,
even if it smells of dog.

The kitchen sink equivalent of
Luke Skywalker – Puke Dishwater –
you are a new hope…
or you would be, if your direct actions
included buying
some organic, fair trade soap.

Wannakah I P21
A character from the wider wankier world of spoken word

Hooligans I P63
Arrested at the age of 15 in an act of post-Hillsborough
over-sensitivity at a football match and branded a
hooligan at school, I penned this.

Slowly, Slowly, Cowley Road I P84
The home of the hippie et al.

The End of the World

Inflatable Buddha song lyrics

The end is nigh,
comes the madman's cry;
your nana watches movies
in black and white.

The end of the world is coming,
but you are not aware –
you're sitting there relaxing in your favourite
chair.

A child puts a frog he's found
in a pan on the stove,
trying to do some mischief before his parents
come home.

The end of the world is coming,
you're starting to perspire,
cos you're sitting there relaxing
too close to the fire.

The movie it is sinister,
a woman and a child,
struggling with the ropes
on the train track where they're tied.

The end of the world is coming,
but you will never learn,
you're sitting there relaxing
as the energy burns.

The water it is boiling,
watched by the child;
the frog he stays quite still,

he can't tell he's gonna die.*

The end of the world is coming,
and though you are quite aware,
you're sitting there
relaxing in your favourite chair.

---

*   This isn't actually true, apparently. It is an urban myth that if you put a frog
    in a pan of cold water and slowly bring it to the boil, the frog will gradually,
    happily boil to death. Still, it serves nicely as a metaphor for the human
    species.

Ape (Not Monkey!) | P37
A song for our close cousins and an online argument that
Disney is worse than porn!

Why Do I Still Live Here? | P106
On this beautiful rainy rock?

Giant | P68
Small poem about climate change

The Electoral Poetry Commission 2015

Written through the night in the studio of BBC Oxford from just before midnight on the 7th of May, for broadcast on the announcement of the result of the general election.

The talk of 2020 vision
becomes memetic –
my guess is that most that
utter it don't get it,
don't see the duality of the fixed term
borrowed from optometry,
but are focused on designs and
the names on the sides,

Brand aware but not engaged.
Ideally votes will be exchanged
for progressive policy
with economic controls,
vanquishing the threats
from the xenophobes,
for the hard-working people
who dig all the holes;
all our futures depend on the Poles(/polls).

The prediction: no one party to be
first past the post,
progressive change a realistic hope,
but...
as the ballot boxes close,
the exit polls toll.

Not 326 but as close as damn it.
The DUP could be the key
for the Eton Rifle to beat
the common enemy.

Right-wing editors rub their hands with glee,
victory for the VE anniversary.
The electorate will be given a decision,
the return of European tunnel vision.

Sunderland sprint to be first one back,
as they take out the one blue vote
and weigh the bag.

Respect for Smith in the intelligent city,
we wait and wait for the inevitable from Witney,
the privileged voice leading
vitriol and distortion,
warping the map and the blue proportion.

Sky's the limit, they believe in better,
social media funding, Tories going meta.

One nation appears to be drifting,
the political tectonic plates are shifting,

landslide from the highlands,
Sturgeon surgin',

too many activists cheering the SNP.
We can't fight against it, says Dimbleby.

Swell for the Greens but no MPs,
votes for UKIP but still no seats,

except all's well for Carswell.
Most halls fill with applause
for reds, yellows, greens, blues, and loons,
but not for followers of pint-swilling Farage;
think UKIP – think boos.

Cable cries, Clegg survives
by the skin of his teeth,
Liberal Democrats completely demolished.
Labour despair at comparisons
to Wallace and Gromit.
It couldn't be much grimmer,
looking at five more years of despair in the *Mirror*.

Boris wins but loses
the chance for a leadership fight,
clowns to the left of him, jokers to the right.

We're left to hover like gannets
for the slender hope
of the result we want to hear from Thanet,

result not yet certain
but speeches tainted with resignation.
The election narrative has been authored
by non-dom millionaire editors
who put progress to the slaughter;
the 2015 election story
was once again written by a Tory.

To May, Whom It Concerns | P115
Adrian Mitchell's 'To Whom It May Concern' rebooted

The Liberal Property Owner | P46
The actual axis of evil

The Midas Touch in Reverse | P20
I'm cursed!

COWLEY RD.
SEE THE PEOPLE CLUTCH CONTROL
SAFETY IN THE GREEN CROSS GLOW
RESTORE THE CALM, LET CYCLES FLOW
SLOWLY ON THE COWLEY ROAD.
NARCOTIC & ORGANIC MEETS
GREENERY & ARTFUL STREETS
EAT THE GLOBE IN ONE SQUARE MILE
BECOME ANOTHER XENOPHILE
STOP A WHILE & SAY HELLO
NAMASTE TO ALL NEPAL.
CZEŚĆ TO ALL THE POLES
WAR & FAMINE IN THE WORLD?
HERE'S YOUR DESTINATION CHILD
ASYLUM WELCOME, INDEPENDENTS !!!
RAISING ASPIRATIONS
ALL ARE WELCOME, ALWAYS HAVE BEEN
WORKHOUSE POOR & THOSE AFFLICTED WITH
DISEASE, DISORDERS & ADDICTIONS
ON SUPPOSED LOWLY COWLEY RD
WHERE GOOD THINGS COME
TO THOSE THAT KNOW
THIS LEPER-HERITAGE
TOLERANCE ZONE
AS HOME.

STEVE LARKIN
.com/cow

choose

82

Can We Be Friends?

Steve Larkin song lyrics

Social constructivist anarchists
blurring the boundaries of politics,
oxymoronic rules they make
and break at their will.

Can we be friends
with a capital 'F'?
Or does this depend
on a rule that we bend?

The boys and the girls are androgynous,
the casual sex is anonymous,
uniformed asymmetric haircuts,
they'll hate you if it's straight.

Can we be friends?
Oi! Can we be friends?
Can we be friends?
Oh! Is this not the trend?

The till in the Mac shop's a genius,
a gimmick that's already tedious.
An affluent man clamours for intimate
experiences on the internet.

Out once a week, think they're gorgeous,
drunk in the wine bars ignored us,
we'll take the spit and the sawdust
and look for alternative routes.

The bar is too high for us to get served,
the drunkenen view is being obscured,
the unresolved gets me motoring.

Can we be friends?
It's a digital trend.
Can we be friends?
Shall we just pretend?

Polly gone sided with Jesu',
Muhammad, for profit, and Vishnu,
Polly gone polyamorous,
time share – yeah – love is when?

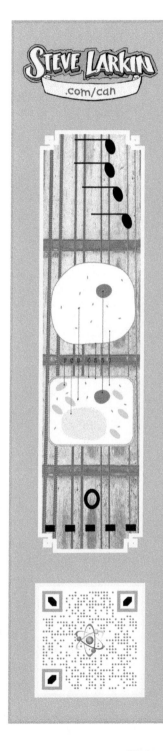

Can we all be friends?
Where will we ascend?
Can we be friends
and meet all our ends?

Discussions of where to set boundaries
made by colliding of histories;
the chances of parties being happy
depends if they attend.

The bar is too high for us to get served,
the drunkenen view is being obscured,
the unresolved gets me motoring,
alternate brushes and contrasting energies.
The black and the white are fading to shades,
the animal within, where we all begin,
society's eyes, society prizes
the prisoner banging at the cell wall;
will the jailor open the door?
Is this a life that we have chosen?
Is this the thrust of fate that's spoken?
Can we be friends
after this artificial end?

What am I to you?
What are you to me?
Forever changing things,
the earth it moves under our feet.

I've travelled the world, the words on my lips:
Je t'adore / Ich leibe dich.
If love's not received, what becomes of it?
Square peg, round hole, no, it won't fit.

The bar is too high for us to get served,
the drunkenen view is being absurd,
the unresolved...

choose

Love Is War | P73
Looks like we can't be friends

If Major Religious Figures Had Lived
Concurrently to Me | P88
An exercise in nothingness

Why Do I Still Live Here? | P106
On this beautiful rainy rock?

Peacocks See Off Terriers*

I remember manning up at Batley Grammar
    School for Boys
to that brash middle-class no-nonsense noise
that big-banged its way down booby-trapped
    corridors,
chock-filled with bollockings
from teachers
whose ear-bashings were more
feared than their canes.
Maddening pointing laughter
at every fall or embarrassment,
echoed by bullish sons of alpha males:
new-moneyed middle managers in an age
of possessive individualist, trickle-down, asset-
    grabbing shite
that saw a bizarre sense of pride
in masculinity, intellectual superiority, Yorkshire,
    and grime.
Gobs fuelled like combustion engines to open
    and shut with loud
glottal-stop insults thrust
at the weak or different
in 'accents clear and proud'.
Top-down didacticism,
make 'em work and punish 'em,
sneering fear the *modus operandum*.
Nicknames abound.

A year of being pecked
and I'm learning the ropes,
being verbally abused
by a kid in my year
when I turn and I face
and I pluck up the courage,
hit back with a reminder of a nickname given,
Fuck off, Alien – you weird-looking ginger,
and he runs at me (a rarity
that a confrontation here involves physicality).
His face is throbbing, pulsating, angry, red,
arms flailing, he's going for my head,

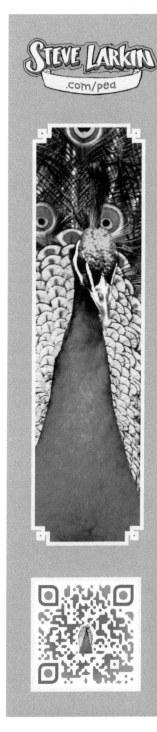

and I push him away as instinct takes over,
and he falls to the floor, gets up, and runs.

And I feel at last like I'm winning the battle,
protecting myself, not letting 'em at me.
And from that day I walk with a swagger,
gob off as I please, and don't fear any bugger,
and I chase after big lads who take our ball,
become a snarling northern bully runt surviving the grammar grind,
a Scrappy-Doo, a yappy dog, an extra from *Kes*, barking offence,
    protecting myself.

And later I learn that that kid that I turned on,
that I so charmingly reminded of his nickname *Alien*,
had been told around that time
that he was adopted
by kind-hearted folks
who added to their brethren,
and when I stood up to whatever petty insult
he had had for me,
it had hit him hard, that reminder
of not belonging to his family,
but for me, in my ignorance, the moment had assisted me,
instilling survival, self-sufficiency, bravery – it had made me.

Years on I see his photos, his boys and his girl,
contented, smiling in their Huddersfield Town shirts,
and I am displaced from my South Leeds roots,
living in a rented room without any family,
strutting my stuff with my angry poetry.

*   Peacocks was/is the nickname of Leeds United Football Club (from the days they spent playing at the Old Peacock Ground – now Elland Road), Terriers is the nickname of Huddersfield Town football club (as in Yorkshire terriers – the yappiest of dogs). The two characters in the piece (who may or may not be based on real-life characters!) are supporters of the two clubs. There is no intended reference to Elizabeth Peacock, who was coincidentally MP for Batley and Spen at the time, but, if you want to apply new historical literary criticism and conclude that this piece demonstrates a subconscious critique of a period in British political history that saw serious damage inflicted on Yorkshire by Thatcher's neo-liberalism, I won't stand in your way!

Woman's Hour Second Breakfast | P54
Introspective poet continues to work – the body extends

Kitten | P36
A true story of a love affair that never happened

We Are the Boys for Fun and Noise | P96
A Larkin poem

If Major Religious Figures Had Lived Concurrently to Me

Buddha would've lived in Milton Keynes, in a two-bedroomed semi with his housemate Steve.

Muhammad would have lived in central London, would've written beautiful poetry and been the bee's knees on the literary scene, and would've been co-opted into some political regime with which he didn't entirely agree.

Jesus would've lived in Glastonbury, would've been a right regular hippy, chaining himself to railings, engaging one and all in forward-thinking, progressive, right-on green schemes.

He would have been largely ignored.

Krishna would've lived all over the country, would've been a loved-up clubber spreading free love and spreading his seed, if the lights were set right and people couldn't see that he was blue.

Ganesh would've lived at the top of the island looking down from John O'Groats, would've caused absolute terror, what with him having an elephant's head an' all.

Yahweh at Darlington – a right cantankerous bastard, would've gated his yard, kept people at a distance whilst he loudly sang his fearsome karaoke favourite: *I Am What I Am.*

All of them would've tried to change people's minds,
tried to convince people of the value of being kind,
whilst asserting a purpose that they held to be divine,
except for Buddha, who would've been happy in his two-bedroomed semi in an egoless new town, calmly espousing the value of nothing to his housemate Steve
– I reckon.

choose

Laugharn's Genius | P90
Dylan Thomas in his natural environment.
An exploration in genius.

The Meaning of Life | P42

One Big Sentence | P61
A thought experiment

Smeg Head

Rolling back the state like your Eton master's foreskin,
did you ever wonder: *where did this begin?*

Those who have trickle-down forced upon them
force trickle-down in return.
When you cut disabled benefits, can you taste the sperm?

A Pavlovian reaction when reverting to a hands-off approach?
The response to deep-set stimuli that makes you thrust it down their
    powerless throats?

Burned into your psyche, as a thing that underpins
your modus operandum and the misery you bring
to the people you forced to their knees.
Seems no degree will help you see
that the bloody cocky bully boys
became the bloody Bullingdon
became the bloody government
to change the bloody state of things,
to fix the game so they would win:

rugger bugger/tennis racquet,
protection for the upper bracket.

Now it's backs against the bloody wall
for everybody, one and all,

who didn't taste the master race
or have an Eton master in their face.

How on earth did our kids get lumbered
with a victim-cum-offender on the numbers? *

_____

*   'On the numbers' is a prison term for a paedophile.

The Liberal Property Owner | P46
The actual axis of evil.

system malfunction | P26
Abandon hope now!

The Day I Fell in Love with a NatWest Service Point | P34
Capitalism - a love story!

Laugharn's Genius

Slept in a town that inspired the creation of Llareggub*
(the reverse of *bugger all*)

to see if the esteemed genius
was still waiting in the wall.**

I listened to *time passing* at the
graveyard by the sea,

strolled by butchers and bakers,
in the hope that ghosts would wake up.

I looked over mudflats and beaches
at white horses in the sea.

I disturbed the bird's poetic repetition,
poetic repetition, repetition…

then I knuckled down to the nuts
and bolts of grammar, nouns, and prepositions.

After a brief local history lesson
where I learned about
abuse of women and substances
and then of the brilliant bard's
vanity publication,
I recommitted to continue my pursuit
of creative poetic expression.

Regardless of the chances of finding an audience
for these potentially ghostly words to be heard,
without awaiting the genius in the wall,
inspired by bugger all.

*If Major Religious Figures Had Lived Concurrently
to Me* | P88
This is what would have happened

Dead Poets' Soc. | P16
Where moaning can be heard emanating from the garret
of the living poet

Peacocks See Off Terriers | P85
Steve Larkin's school days

She Said

She said:
Your arrogance makes you bad in bed.

And he said:
Well, you still seem to let me
like you did when you first met me.

And she said:
I only wanted… you know…
and you were quite good-looking.

And he said:
I know… and I know you didn't
mean it when…
when you said I was bad in bed…
cos I've seen the way you shudder
from your toes to your head.

And she said:
Do you think I'm so stupid
that I can't pretend?

And he said:
Yes, I do…
I do.

There was an awkward silence
of a minute or two.
He looked into the air
and she stared at her shoes,
until she plucked up some courage
and raised up her head,
and she said:
Can you tell me what exactly
you are trying to do?
Can you tell me what exactly
you are trying to prove?
Convince me that I'm stupid,
I'll come running to you?
Well, ain't that the truth? Cos I do…
I do…
I do.

She said:

Your passive aggression
really screws with my head.

And he said:

———

Till she said:
I hope you don't expect to get in my bed again.

And he said:
You know as well as me
that it's a matter of when.
Don't pretend, I'm your last chance
or you'll end up on the shelf.

And she said:
You've really got a knack of knowing how to offend.

And he said:
I know...
I do...
I do.

There was an awkward silence
of an hour or two.
He switched on the telly for something to do.
She went into the kitchen to dry off her eyes,
then she returned to the room,
and she said:
You should have left here
about an hour ago,
you know it's half past ten,
you know it'll happen again...
we'll end up in bed,
and then I'll wake up in the morning,
and I'll feel like nothing...
and you'll walk out that door
with that smug expression...
like you're number one
cos you nailed me again...
it's like a nail in the coffin of my self-respect...
of my self-esteem...
look what you're doing to me...
your arrogance makes you bad in bed...
your arrogance makes you bad in bed...
your arrogance makes you bad in bed.

Well, that crack about his arrogance
had dented his pride.
The challenge was set:
tonight he'd show her the night of her life!

And the less said
about that night in her bed,
the better.
The less said
about that night in her bed,
the better.
The less said about that night
in her bed, the better?

Four years on
she's stood at the church.
She sees the aisle.
She sees the altar.
And she sees him.
And it makes her think:
I'll alter him.

A few moments later,
a song and a sermon,
and she's uttered the words,
bound herself till death
to honour and serve,

because she said
(as one in twenty women said when asked),
she said that she had been raped,
not by a stranger,
not by a friend,
but by somebody other;
she said that she had been raped…
by her lover.
She said:
I do.

Oi, Codger! | P99
Commissioned piece that aims to encourage people
to take up exercise

Smeg Head | P89
Another power imbalance story

Peacocks See Off Terriers | P85
Steve Larkin's school days

The 1st

The alarm, the squeaky bed, the present, the card.
You're 36! Impeccable maths!
1980, the year that God made me –
the perennial apposite earworm chorus
runs through my head again,
quieter this year, then it fades.

Another happy return will occur later on –
the frog to the pond from where it was spawned.
We'll drive the route from city to village:
the church, the graveyard,
strewn with the beauty
of the colour of the fallen leaves.

And we'll absorb the warmth –
those kindly wrinkling faces
raising cold glasses
in their decadent outdoor retirement hot tub –
a heavenly pool with a beautiful view.
And, clutching the flutes
with our own wrinkling fingers,
we'll field blatant, subtle
and unconscious questions
in the talk about the family extension.

And we will return,
back to the city,
to our two-bed terrace,
where we'll peddle our art,
go to work on the cycle,
compost the leaves in the garden,
ensure that we clean up our nest,
and we'll tighten the nuts in this bed that we lie in,
and quietly become gods ourselves.

Peacocks See Off Terriers | P85
My teachers and other animals

Dead Poets' Soc. | P16
A living poet moans!

Incubator | P113
The world's most ambitious chat-up line: Will you
be an incubator for my DNA?

We Are the Boys for Fun and Noise

This poem was written for my granddad Jack Larkin Snr's ninetieth birthday, and it's a celebration of him and the family he raised. He and a friend of his won a talent contest with a song of the same title in the 1930s. The poem is rammed full of in-jokes and references that outsiders to the family won't understand. However, much can be inferred and people seem to like it, so it's included in the collection.

My favourite line is an idiom that the great man said to me once when I told him many years ago that I'd been made redundant but didn't much care for the job anyway; I'd get another. He responded with the line, 'Aye, tha's plenty of brass in tha' face,' which to me was a brilliant application of lay poetry.

If this poem serves only to preserve that phrase, I'll be happy.

We are the boys for fun and noise,
big-headed, big-handed bundles of joys.
We are the boys for fun and noise,
banging out rhythms since we could hold toys.

We are the boys for music and mirth;
the women were screaming from the time of our births,
cos we are the big-headed, big-handed males,
makers of good times and lagers and ales.

We are the boys for fun and noise;
we speak to be heard in our proud Yorkshire voice,
good for the grammar, rolling our R's,
mess with our kid and you're on your arse.

We are the boys for music and mirth,
bitter drinkers, the salt of the earth,
in our baggy trousers and dirty shirts,
banging out a big booming belching curse.

We are the boys for making a racket,
hammering, drilling, fixing a bracket,
racing, making or breaking a bicycle,
delivering organic veg on a cargo tricycle.

We are the boys for marking occasions
with musical performances and standing ovations.
We are the big-skulled brains full of dates,
remembering the birthdays of family and mates.

We are the boys full of energy and noise,
with big blue batteries strapped to our toys;
piss-taking, leg-pulling jokes we enjoy,
the givers and takers of a thousand *doyyys*.

We are the life and soul of the pub,
who pay up the subs to prop up the club,
mouthing the bassline to 'Taxman'/the Jam,
pounding out rhythm on what comes to hand.

We are the boys for fun and rhymes,
for good times in harsh climes;
we'll take what we find.
We're T*rin' till We Die/Marching on Together.*
No matter if tha's running on a shoelace,
cos there's plenty of brass in tha' face:

Black Dyke to Black Grape,
'White Christmas', White Stripes,
rock 'n' roll, Teddy Boy, rocksteady,
psychedelic, punk rock,
klezmer ska, Radioheads,

tuned-in fanatics, in fact
every question we can answer.
We are the pop masters,
we are the boys for fun and noise.

From the vibrating strings of the
Godfather's mandolin,
a love of fun and music continuing
through Generation X to Y and Z,
we'll never be dead
if we make music and mirth;
the rhythm method will mean more births.

Yes, we are the boys for fun and noise,
big-headed, big-handed bundles of joys,
not afraid to blow our own trumpets,
and if you want to know
what the sound of an extra-long trump is,
you won't be waiting long,
cos we are brewing, creating, making, crass, laughing, joke-telling,
funny-faced farting Larkins.

We are the boys for,
we are the girls for,
we are the boys for –
1, 2, 3, 4 –
we are the boys for fun and noise!

choose

Oi, Codger! | P99
Encouraging older people to take up exercise

Sonny – Prestatyn | P105
A Philip Larkin poem rebooted

The 1st | P95
Next-generation Larkin.

Oi, Codger (Be a Better Coffin Dodger!)

This poem was commissioned by the Community Foundation and first read in the Houses of Parliament at the launch of a campaign that encouraged older people to take up some form of exercise in order to stay healthy and socially connected.

Wrinkly?
Retired?
Seem like an age since you last perspired?

Old?
Cold?
Sat by a radiator reminiscing about coal?

Pension not stretching?
Counting the cost?
Face like a bulldog chewing a wasp?

Face getting wrinkled?
Pallid and tired?
Got more lines than a
very naughty schoolchild?

Isolated?
No phone calls?
Feeling a bit deflated
like an old leather football?

Well – pump it up!
Pump it up, wrinkly!
Get up, stand up!
Stand up for your life!

Get the blood pumping!
Get oxygen to your skin!

You've lived too long
in black and white;
let's let some colour in!

Let your rosy cheeks defy

the time you've been alive!

That cardiovascular
regenerates over distance
if you give it time!

So be young at heart!
Give yourself a kickstart!
Get your motor running!
Get out on your bike, mate!

Sick of *Countdown*, tea and talking?
Get your hiking boots on –
start walking.
Don't turn into a miserable old codger;
be a better coffin dodger.
If you start trekking
you'll live long and prosper!

Been on your own since your good wife's demise?
Dementia taking you back to the
days on the prowl with the guys?
You wanna meet women?
Go swimming!
There are rows and rows of blue-rinse honeys
in lines in lanes keeping trim in their bikinis,
and while you're at the pool
you won't have to pay for central heating!

Yes – the sound of the word *cuts* grates.
Yes – the sum that won't add up
makes your heart palpitate,
your pupils dilate,
and your head ache,
but... worrying?
That's not the best way
to increase your heart rate, mate,
and you don't want to be late
for the human race,
so don't sit at home cold and alone,
osmosing injustice
from your head to your toes,
injecting your bloodstream with cortisol;
get your skates on and go.
And relax! Go do it!
Increase longevity!

Remember the prayer that brings serenity:
accept the things you cannot change,
change the things you can.
Push back the bile for a while, smile,
and dance!
Take a partner by the hand;
there may be trouble ahead,
but while there's mucus, and blood types,
and food, and no grants,
let's play the music and dance!

And if you can't stand,
just wave your hands

(all you wrinklies who independent).

Can't walk for long?
Stay home; play ping pong!
One arm working? Whiff whaff?
Don't matter you think Boris is a toff… twit!

If you're thinking of giving up the ghost
and giving up the garden
for an easily maintained bit of crazy paving,
keep a little patch, get digging,
and get delaying the laying of that final stone.
And don't be alone;
get out and get social.
You've lived and worked too long
to be bored and glum.
Life's a party and we're all invited!
At the end the agenda should be fun!

So, wannabe codger,
don't be a lonely retirement home lodger;
exercise your right to be alive through… exercise!
Steal some time, fly the wrinkly Jolly Roger,
don't be a quiz show countdown clock-watcher,
and be a better coffin dodger!

 Sonny – Prestatyn | P105
A Philip Larkin poem rebooted

 The 1st | P95
Next-generation Larkin

 RIP Steve Larkin | P120
Steve Larkin is dead

The Only Truths I've Ever Known

The only truths I've ever known are those that
    I have spoken.
Innate/self-evident, in my DNA, or nurtured
    by experience and awoken?
The only truths I've ever known are those that
    I have spoken.
And when solidified by utterance they could
    not be broken –
incantatem, spellbound, certain, the paths
    that I had chosen.
The only truths I've ever truly known are those
    that I have spoken.

Those inky blots I struggled to osmose,
the minim split spilt on the stave,
the code with no emotion,
were dots and tails from dominant males
that in me could not germinate
until there came the chance to play,
to beat the skin myself and pound
the rhythmic rock that was the ground,

on which I built corporeal sounds,
the waves on which I sailed around,
and when I got my mouth around
sweet melody, the sense I found.

Stimulation then abounded when I unleashed
    the meaning bound in neural paths
that when unwound released the truth that I
    could lash my tongue to –

the only songs that I've retained are those
    that I have sung along to.

I marched the playground as a child
to earn the right to one day fly,
and all I can recall to date is
right wheel, left wheel, eyes right, halt.
No mechanics of the plane I flew;
just the drill master's racket

that banged its way inside my head
became the thing I 'knew'.

And when it came to understanding,
'twas bound intrinsically to repeating;
not *two legs bad, four legs good* and vice versa,
as other contented pigs might order,
but from a position of a profoundly discontented porker,
unearthing lies like truffles in the dirt, to challenge those that ought to
open ears and minds to that which I had lorded over with forceful
reason to make the truth be outed loudly.

The truths that I have known the most are those that I have shouted,
in rooms of friends and strangers captured by the lure and lie of
      entertainment or cultures that surround it –
the only truths I've ever learned are those that I have heard,
      conceived, repeated.
When attempting to absorb that that dripped from others' mother
      tongues,
I'd dry up until the time would come to *écoutez et répétez*,
and only when my mouth chewed them round with an increase in
      viscosity
would any neologism stick and find a home in me.

The only instances in which I've really appreciated any other's
      substances
have occurred when they have moved me with their vocal utterances.

When an inarticulate mild, meek, modest lover from whom I'd parted
met with me to pick the bones of what we'd started,
and I took breath, to give her rest from incessant desperate probing,
and she looked me in the eyes and whimpered,
I miss you,
only then did I truly know her feelings.

And no length of love letter, greetings-card gushing
or elongated email explanation
could do justice to the love she showed me in that one moment.

The only truths I've ever known are those that have been spoken.

So stick the rigidity of your dictionary denotations
and the self-impregnated, self-important written culture that's
      exploded
from a printing press that mass-produced a narrow view of what was
      true to a fifteenth-century goldsmith.

The truth is formed by what I've heard and what I've said,
it oscillates inside my head,
it will continue to until I'm dead,
and when I've gone and rotted down
to bones, or dust, and stone or bust,
the only access to the truths that I've proposed
will be from direct witnesses who were present when I spoke.
And I hope when those who found themselves within my sonic range
    have the same enquiry as me,
they will assent that truth is assembled in the blend of conception
    and speech.

In utterance,
in utero.

The meat machine,
computer code.

In utterance,
in utero.

Your governance
of cogito.

In utterance,
in utero.

Breathe to life,
new births,
behold:

The only truths you've ever known are those that you have spoken.

choose

I Hate Poetry Please | P31
Yes! I am convinced by your spoken word manifesto, now
please trash other approaches to presenting poetry!

Lemming Me Wrong | P69
No! Enough telling me what to think. Give me something
with a more imagist approach and gaps I can fill in myself.
Make it dark!

The London Eye | P51
Anarchic ranting tourist guide on his first and very last
day in the job

Sonny - Prestatyn

This is a modern-day rewrite of Philip Larkin's 'Sunny Prestatyn'. It would be good to read the original first if you are unfamiliar with it.

The Cancer Research Google ad
pops up in the corner in blue.
The irony would make you cry
if you knew how he lost his life.
The mustachioed lips of his smile
remain if you swipe right.
Navigate further in, behold!
You can witness him holding

a tuberous cock and balls,
that sets him apart from
Titch – Llandudno.
High scores – well in! This is the space,
he thought, a way to fill the void.
No more lonely rural nights since
he made a 'dating' profile that he
slapped up one day in March.

He spread himself thinly for a while,
joy expanding from his muscly thighs.
In hotels with his large palms,
he became the hunk on the coast,
guaranteed to satisfy, kneeling on the sand,
and now he's just an image that excites
those who, ignorant of his demise,
cum to Sonny – Prestatyn.

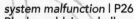

system malfunction I P26
Bleak worldview challenge. Don't expect to be any
happier at the end – and it is the end, isn't it?

I Met a Girl I P72
The inadvertent morality lessons a serial
monogamist receives

Laugharn's Genius I P90
Dylan Thomas in his natural environment.
An exploration in genius

Why Do I Still Live Here?

Why do I still live here,
under these grey unforgiving skies,
where I will live and die?
We're at the start of the year,
at the top of the world,
tilted into the darkness
and feeling unfulfilled.
Then the buds come out,
and the blossom spreads around,
and the just exchange their messages in the
        summer festival tent,
but then a dark cloud grows,
looms above my head.

Why do I still live here,
under these wet and aggressive skies,
where I may never get dry?
Where millions marching for justice
prove to be ignored.
Now it's raining down uranium
like it's raining down on the poor.
The few that profit from suffering
are ahead of the property curve.
Value added across the board,
but no one told the pawns.
In lieu of revolutionary zeal,
I'm forced to ask myself:

Why do I still persist
voting with two-party politricks
where I don't get to decide?
Where, woven into the fabric –
bloodstained loser hope,
glory to the fallen,
if they fall in front of the goal.
Those that pay the penalty,
the stunned and silenced majority,
scraping saving all the years
that a home loss is their fear,
fed just enough to stay alive,
but also force-fed lies.

Why do I still get mad
at those that don't seem to mind the gap,
even though they're constantly told?
So emigrate or start a revolution!
Or live in a geodesic dome
in a commune near Frome!
Sing your songs, hope they sing along,
and add to the noise pollution,
and cry:
Why?!
Why – do I – still live here?

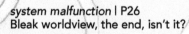

Black Friday

Way too early for a poet, on the morning of 13 November 2015 Steve Larkin was invited into the studio of BBC Oxford to be presented with a subject to write a poem about in a short space of time. The poem was to be presented live on air. The preamble involved a conversation that went along the lines of:

Presenter: *So you're a poet; do you make a living out of that?*

Poet: *Well, I eke a living. For many years my dad would start any phone conversation with 'So, are you earning a crust?' like he didn't believe that it could be a valid profession.*

The subject given was the news article about fashion retail park Bicester Village's decision to opt out of bargain shopping day Black Friday after the previous year's carnage. This poem was the result of a barely conscious, sleep-deprived brain's struggle with time constraints and the real world.

Clogging up the roads,
arteries blocked,
the flow stops,
like black pudding.

A coagulating disease,
perspective lost,
counting the reducing cost,
like the Black Death.

Bring out your dead,
don't let it spread,
Bicester starts the revolution,
like the Black Panthers.

But from Lanarkshire to Hampshire
the cheap things shine at the end of the week;

the roads will be rocked
before the Black Sabbath.

A poet carves verse
about the bargain basement.
This is the death of entertainment,
like Black Lace,

the poetry equivalent of 'Agadoo'.
I'm sorry, Dad, it's what I do.

And, what's worse,
Black Friday doesn't even work;
it's bust and boom
before the inevitable absurd advertising chorus of *Have a Merry
    Christmas with B&Q!*
Black Friday – a short-termism-spawning, global-warming-*causing,
    treading-on-your-neighbour's head, a-four-by-four-on-Santa's-
    sled, pushing-a-pensioner-to-her-knees-for-a-few-quid-off-a-
    cheap-TV shopping day pandering to wanton greed.*

Meanwhile – *Children in Need!*

Electoral Poetry Commission 2015 | P79
Political piece for BBC radio

If Major Religious Figures... | P88
An exercise in nothingness.

A Contrived Poem... | P117
Have a Merry Christmas... with B&Q!

Live in Trees

Live in trees,
live in trees,
live suspended in beauty from
branches of ash, cedar, or beech.

Live in trees,
live in trees,
live in low-impact dwellings
as part of eco-centric communities.

Live anywhere that's a far cry from the neat,
    clean, plundering streets,
Amazon-gleaning, with drains bleeding
bleach.

Live in trees cos they're gorgeous.
Live in trees cos they're strong.
Spend your time farming food
    and playing the fool,
because that's all you'll have to do.

Live in trees,
live in trees,
live in trees,
please!

Live in trees,
live in trees,
live in small woodland clearings,
live in straw bales, benders, and yurts.

Live in trees,
live in trees,
take on the green ethos of sustainable beliefs,
the only ones in reach of all of those too poor
    to afford a piece of concrete.

Live in trees that give oxygen.
Live in trees that stop floods.
Get a panel on your roof,
let your loo feed the roots,
sleep soundly with bugs in your rugs.

Live in trees,
live in trees,
live in trees,
please!

Do your best,

and when you've left
jostling head-aching commuter belt death
you'll understand acutely why you are blessed
to be free of inner-city debates of race and hate
as your peers focus energy on sharing wealth.

When people ask about living in the canopy,
when you travel back to the bonds of Babylon
for the weddings and funerals of your former brethren,
you'll paint them a picture that is close to utopia –
life surrounded by the living more fulfilling than ennui in leafy
    suburbia.
When you consider your world as you stare at the stars
in your hammock by the fire as it warms up your thighs,
you'll sigh about the time that it took you to find
the reconnection with the earth and your primal desires.

When people ask about living in trees,
you'll ask them to join
because there's no need for greed
when life exists so mutually and beneficially,
when I support the tree and the tree supports me,
when I give it gases every time I speak
and it then produces the very air that I breathe.
You'll preach because it's a completely fulfilling relationship being a
    new man or new woman in a natural co-dependent cycle of life,
    watching the fat fruit growing ripe, eating it, and then fertilising
    its seeds…

So…

Live in trees,
live in trees,
enjoy your time
hanging with the people that you meet.

Live in trees,

live in trees,
climb to the top of an actual tree with leaves,

and just remember that you're just passing through
your part of this life, but it's not all about you –

use your brain and think,
and think about biology, politics, ecology
and the traps that get set for the masses of oppressed.

If you want to be clever, and classless, and free,
if you want to be clever, and classless, and free,
if you want to be clever, and classless, and free,
become a fucking peasant living up a tree.

choose

Ape (Not Monkey!) | P37
Live in trees because you're an ape, you know.
And you're Great!

Striking Chords | P44
Me and my mandolin, who makes me sing.

RIP Steve Larkin | P120
Steve Larkin is dead

Incubator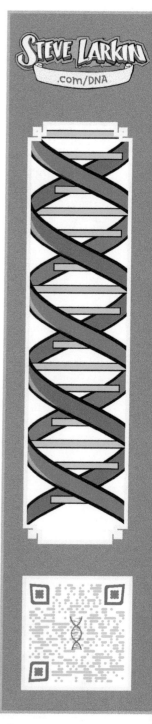

Will you be an incubator for my DNA?
Because if you'll be my wine glass, I'll be your
    cabernet.
The fruit's fermenting, it needs bottling,
it needs a clean environment... for it to blossom in.
Will you be the vessel of reproduction for my
    encoded molecule of genetic instruction,
    baby?
There's merely a smattering of insanity in the
    history of my family,
so be the conduit for my genetic code?
Be the fertile ground
where my seed can grow?
Will you be my baby momma?
Come on, baby, say you're gonna offer your
    fallopians, so a new custodian
can move into your womb.

Will you be the incubator for my DNA?
Darling! Store my nucleic acid,
be its breeding place.
I can't promise much:
a sensitive touch
(when it comes to the fun conceiving stuff),
a nurturing instinct, a big safe pair of hands
(that are mostly in proportion with all the other
    organs and glands),
a life expectancy of at least nine months
and eighteen years,
and a scream-detecting pair of grabbable ears.

Will you be the incubator for my DNA?
Give it warmth and nutrients and help it on its way?
I've been through childhood, puberty,
adolescence,
and adulthood for so long now that I'm bored of
    life's repeating lessons.
So be the paper for the blueprint of our self-
    replicating patterns –
make me a new human being, my love, by making
    me a new human being, my love.
If you do, I promise to keep its orifices clean, my

113

love,
warm up the nipples
whenever it needs a feed, my love,
take it for walks and teach it to read, my love,
pass on my wisdom and give it all my love, my love.

Will you be the incubator for my DNA?
Extend your pretty labia for the new head of our family, bear the
    childbirth pain?
Allow me to offer stimulation
that will open your cervix for my ejaculation
because I'm getting good at copulation.
Come, consent to be my gestation station,
take a break from menstruation.
Let's get to work on impregnation.
Take a slide down my double helix.
Take a chance on my unique sequence.
Write the text of you-and-me the sequel.
See what you plus me will really equal.

If you endure the morning sickness, the heavy weight,
the bulbous shape,
the screaming pain, and the excruciating splitliness,
I promise to fill our family's days with security and happiness.
If you'll be the grow bag for my DNA strand,
and squeeze a human through your foof,
then I promise I'll hold your hand.

Thank Fuck | P50
It's short!

Kitten | P36
A true story of a love affair that never happened

Curtains | P45
Love and marriage go together like poetry
and cynicism.

To May, Whom It Concerns
(Tell Me Lies About… Everything)

This poem was a commission from the Royal Albert Hall for performance at their 'Beat Poetry Rebooted' event, which took poetry from the 1965 International Poetry Incarnation event as a starting point for new writing. I took Adrian Mitchell's 'To Whom It May Concern (Tell Me Lies About Vietnam)' and applied it to the contemporary political scene just in advance of the 2017 general election.

I was always taught to tell the truth, Mrs May,
and since I was a child I've carried on that way,
    so gnaw at me with soundbites
    and tell me lies about… everything.

Heard the gutter-press utterances screaming indignation,
found a way to pull the plug and let it flow away again,
    so fill my paths with common enemies,
    turn me against my neighbour,
    tell me lies about immigration.

Every time I go outside all I hear is blame,
and at matriculation all I hear are Norman names –
    so fill your benches with Übermenschen,
    there's room at the top, please tell me still,
    and don't forget to fake-smile as you kill,
    and tell me lies about social mobility.

I smell burning chlorine, hope it's just the Middle East.
They're only being civil, it's not for us to intervene –
    so sell your bombs to despots,
    sell your guns to kids,
    arm and justify the terrorists,
    and tell me lies about domestic security.

Where were you at the time of the crime,
when the power was ceased to appease the far

right?
Edging your bets with a soft Remain –
    so now jingle jangle jingoism,
    soapbox, tubthump for the middle,
    point at those who you say meddle,
    tell me lies about the European Union.

You put your election date in,
you put your bomb posters out,
you find your major donors,
spread your tax breaks about…

So confuse me with some Latin,
correct my kids with grammar,
let them have a damn good thwacking,
give my land away for fracking,
champion hunts and rule the waves,
start and end for all in Wargrave.
Change the boundaries,
change the rules,
repeat, repeat, repeat untruths,
give me *déjà vu*.
Fill me full of fudge
and tell me lies about obesity,
tell me lies about child poverty
with the central lie of a strong economy,
tell me lies about the National Health
and the newfound international wealth,
tell me lies about political stability,
tell me lies about our increased security,
tell me lies about your political adversaries,
make this island hostile territory… to the truth.

Tell me lies about your motivation
for listening to our conversations.
Are you listening, Mrs May?
Are you listening?

Tell me lies about everything.

Electoral Poetry Commission 2015 | P79
Political piece for BBC radio

Black Friday | P108
Way too early on BBC Breakfast.

Wash More | P74
Please!

A Really Contrived Poem  About Contrived Occasions That I Have Contrived for the Contrived Occasion of National Poetry Day

Have a Merry Christmas – with B&Q!
What better way to celebrate
the birth of our Lord
than with cut-price deals on plasterboard?

British Valentine's Sirloin Steak –
because nothing says *I love you*
more than the thrifty supermarket
butchery of a cow.
Thank you, good St Valentine and Morrisons,
for a steak for just two pounds.

Halloween around the corner?
Get this frightening Ann Summers nurse outfit
    for just a tenner.
Get to fuck, you think – yes, that seems to be
    the message:
you'll get to, if you invest in some Halloween
    faux leather!

Where's this all going to lead?
Get your mead for Eid?
A manicure for Hanukkah?
DVDs of Joe Pasquale for Diwali?
A gastric band for Ramadan?
Nude calendar for Advent?
Vodka set for Lent?

What? No connection between product/service
and celebration?
No worries; we'll make up a poem for all
occasions –
to grammar we'll pay proper no attention;
we'll force some rhymes and then just disregard
scansion.

117

Cos you'll need a card!
You'll need a card!
Like a puppy we'll remind you:
a card's not just for Christmas – ay?
There's a *new* occasion every day!

Happy Uncle and/or Aunty Day, Pete and Karen,
I got you this card that says *Sorry You Were Barren!*

A combo special:
Happy Retirement/Sympathy
to old Brian from pensions and his wife.
He always did encourage us to plan ahead in life.

What you gonna get for your Tinder date?
A T-shirt that ironically states
I went out with xxx
and all I got was chlamydia
from the disappointing sex?

Baby shower? Shower of shite!
For your *fill in blank,*
I got you *this pile of wank,*

sold to me with OCB,
Occasion-Based Marketing
infecting me from the age of three
with Coca-Cola Santa's jingle-jangle.
The white-haired man fixed it for me
and all the other guys and gals.
We never really stood a chance
when a critical mass of morons
made it the norm,
banging the drum for pointless dances
so people repeated freakish mantras:
Have a Merry Christmas with B&Q – fuck you!
I've had a vision of your future.
Your bloated body is cast adrift on a floating blob of toxic rot in the
        middle of a nuclear sea, being sodomised by a mutant chicken
        escaped from an oceanic chain of KFCs,
    its talons rubbing your face in the chocolate wrappers, soiled nappies
        and rusty razor blades beneath, as it holds you down to ram you

with its novelty plastic prosthetic cock made in the shape of the branded beak.

And you? You are asking for the go-large happy family meal deal – because it's cheap.

Anyway, Dad, Happy Father's Day.
Sorry I never sent you a card.

Smeg Head | P89
They fuck you up, those bully boys

Peacocks See Off Terriers | P85
They fuck you up, those bully boys

Funny Old Game | P47
They cut you up, those pacey strikers/existentialist philosophers.

RIP Steve Larkin

Here lies Steve Larkin,
who hated cut flowers.
So don't go leaving them here
like some distasteful reminder
of the ephemeral nature
of his disappointed life.

He hated much about them:
the carbon footprint, the monoculture,
the sentimentality, the pesticides.
But more than the cheap, wrapped-in-plastic,
last-minute petrol forecourt afterthought,
magnifying the fact that life's beauty
will fade and die,
it was the fact that a sexual being
could so easily, ritualistically,
be cut down in its prime.

So plant a seed,
let it grow from his head,
let his grasp exceed
the fact that he's dead.

 Sonny – Prestatyn I P105
The other dead Larkin.

 .TV I P15
Other people's deaths.

 The Meaning of Life I P42

Acknowledgements

I'd like to thank Arts Council England for the generous funding that bought time and resources to produce this book and the associated online material. Bless her and all who feed on her nourishing teats!

It is no straightforward task embarking on creating a written publication when one's life and career have led one down a path of almost pure performance. I wasn't entirely sure that it was worth the effort for a while. I am indebted to a great number of 'critical friends' who were a vital part of the process. The process included sending versions of pieces that were candidates for inclusion and asking for detailed feedback as to their qualities, and particularly their value, if any, on the page. This group of skilful writers convinced me of the value of the material included in this collection. They helped me to shape what it has become. They are:

A.F. Harrold, Luke Wright, Alison Brackenbury, Richard Smith aka Elvis Mcgonagall, Rob Gee, David Holloway aka Mr Social Control, Kersti Worsley, Rebecca Tantony, Tina Sederholm, Tom Parry, Jim Thomas, Mark Gwynne Jones, Gerry Potter, Chris Beschi aka Poetcurious, Michael Parker, and Sophia Blackwell.

Huge thanks goes to the creative powerhouse that is A.F. Harrold, who used his considerable skill and judgement, as well as his valuable time, to edit the book. He is a beautiful and generous human. Special mention also to Rob Gee who took on more than his fair share of editing and feedback with this project, I am grateful for the constant source of inspiration, encouragement, and advice over many years.

I am indebted to the many performance spaces and people who make that world go round for the opportunities to try out and record pieces: Matt Sage and the Catweazle Club; Sophia Blackwell and Blacks Club, Soho; Hammer & Tongue Solent – Matt West, Damian O'Vitch, Jayne Ede et al.; Hammer & Tongue Cambridge – Fay Roberts *et al.*; Hammer & Tongue Bristol – Thommie Gillow *et al.*; Hammer & Tongue Oxford; Neil Spokes and Tina Sederholm; all at Vancouver, Winnipeg, Victoria, Calgary and Edmonton Fringe Festivals, the North Wall Arts Centre, Hugh Warwick and Wood Festival, Adam Riley and Toby Yoga and all at the Firry Mic.

Thanks to performers who allowed me to gatecrash their shows to perform and record the odd piece, such as Luke Wright and Simon Munnery.

Thanks to Ricky Tart, Neil Spokes, Pete Hunter and Chris Baines for video work. To Nigel Firth for audio recording and tech, to Paul Richardson for impressive archiving and for conjuring recordings made eons ago, to Martin Rushent (RIP) for his 'creative fucking genius'. To my musical collaborators who gave permission to use their work and who helped shape and record pieces – the members of Inflatable Buddha – Su Jordan, Dave Hart, Mauro Sanin, Alex Horwill, Rupert Allison, James Schumann, and Richard Brotherton, and to Sam Hinchliffe for the piece 'Man Fights Machine and Loses', which helps make 'Love Is War' worthwhile.

John Seagrave aka Jonny Fluffypunk for conversations that helped me form the idea for the book. Massive thanks to all at Burning Eye – to Clive Birnie (who accepted a way less than straight-forward publication project) and the team that put in the extra mile to accommodate my pernickety insistence on particularities of performance poetry presentation: Bridget Hart, Harriet Evans, and to Liv Torc (who did a gargantuan shift on design and typesetting).

Huge gratitude to the enormously talented Joshua Squashua for the cover design. And also to Stig for design advice and for the use of examples of his work, which includes just a fraction of the work that he's done to support many of my endeavors over decades.

To Victoria Larkin for being an ear whether she wanted to be or not!

And to all the ears over the years that drew these words from my mouth in an act of creative osmosis. This book is your fault!

Encore!

There is more to see from Steve Larkin. Please follow the links below for:

N.O.N.C.E. – video of spoken word theatre show about working as a 'poet-in-residence' with convicted murderers and rapists in a therapeutic prison.

stevelarkin.com/non

Poetry or Death by Terror – TEDx talk in defence of publicly funded art.

stevelarkin.com/ted

TES: Tess of the D'Urbervilles Reimagined – video of spoken word theatre show with 3D binaural audioscape (in production).

stevelarkin.com/tes

New poems – produced after this book went to print

stevelarkin.com/new

Tunes! – Inflatable Buddha pieces and new bits of music.

stevelarkin.com/tunes

Image Credits

Cover design - #squashua - instagram.com/squashua.artist/?hl=en

Video camera outline - dion_dresschers - https://www.needpix.com/photo/1297844/icon-video-camera

Mic with man silhouette - OpenClipart-Vectors - pixabay.com/vectors/karaoke-logo-microphone-singer-man-160752/

Clapperboard - Clcker-free-vector-images - pixabay.com/vectors/clapperboard-film-movie-cut-311792/

'Dead Poets' Soc.' – from Angel of Grief by Bert G Kaufmann - flickr. com/photos/22746515@N02/25627837694/\ + in QR code - Robin Williams - Thierry Ehrmann flickr.com/photos/ home_of_chaos/15340677495

'Wannakah' – from Kanye West Sydney Opera House by Joseph Younis - flickr.com/photos/strike1/122529970/

'The Day I..." Piggy Heart Love Funny - Alexas_Fotos - pixabay.com/photos/piggy-bank-h...love-funny-1592624/

'Kitten' – Angel Kitten - birgl - pixabay.com/photos/cat-angel-christmas-wing-kitten-3869583/ + margin Steve Larkin fish Eye - Jean Paldan

'Post-Colonial Global Blues' – blue-ocean-blue-planet-city-920300(1) Photo by Joseph Redfield from Pexels

'System Malfunction' – City Storm Max Pixel - maxpixel.net/Damage-City-Storm-Natural-Disaster-Transportation-3253414

'Original Sin' - from live sketch at Firry Mic by Merlin Porter - merlinporter.wordpress.com

'I Hate Poetry Please' - adapted from commons.wikimedia.org/wiki/File:Edgar_Bergen_and_Mortimer_Snerd_1941.JPG

'Ape' Pink Blass Slapping Gorilla by Will Fisher https://www.flickr.com/photos/fireatwillrva/5940826577/

'The Meaning...' - The Thinker - Alexandra Bakun - pixabay.com/
photos/thinker-statue-thoughtfulness-1810929/

'Fat Sex' – Fat Sex Show Image by Stig - shtiggy.wordpress.com/

'Funny Old Game' - Jimmy Greaves https://it.wikipedia.org/wiki/
File:Jimmy_Greaves_-_1961_-_AC_Milan.jpg + Albert Camus -
commons.wikimedia.org/wiki/File:Albert-camus.jpg

'London Eye' - Dimitris Vetsikas - https://pixabay.com/photos/
london-eye-ferris-wheel-london-3931237/

'Idiot's Guide...' - Soother/Pacifier - Clker-Free-Vector-Images

https://pixabay.com/vectors/pacifier-soother-dummy-
comforter-308505/

'Live in Leeds' - Victoria Quarter - Michael Beckwith - pixabay.com/
photos/victoria-quarter-county-arcade-2602042/

'One Big Sentence' - Earth - WikiImages - pixabay.com/photos/ earth-
blue-planet-globe-planet-11009/ + Bike Wheel - Clker-Free- Vector-
Images - pixabay.com/vectors/wheel-tire-bicycle-round- bike-307316/
+ Noose - Clker-Free-Vector-Images - pixa-bay.com/ vectors/noose-
hangman-hanging-knot-312261/

'Hooligans' - #squashua- from cover design - instagram.com/
squashua.artist/?hl=en

'Melody' - adapted from River portrait - Brian Tomlinson - flickr.com/
photos/brian_ tomlinson/36982227545

'I Met a Girl' - Celebrate Earth Nature Sun Moon - John Hain - pixa-
bay.com/illustrations/celebrate-earth-nature-sun-moon-954794/

'Love is War' - Bombing Love - Operation Paper Storm - flickr.com/
photos/thinkanonymous/5287505939 + Margin - 'Steve Larkin -
Heavy Gun' - adapted from James Sutton photo - https://www.
facebook.com/jamesalexanderphotographer/

'Wash More' - Che - OpenClipart-Vectors - pixabay.com/vectors/che-
guevara-red-silhouette-stripes-158841/

'End of the World' - from Boiling the Frog by purpleslog - flickr.com/photos/purpleslog/2881603057 +

'Slowly, Slowly, Cowley Road' - photo of mural by Mani www.thebigorangeM.com

'Can We Be Friends' Differences between simple animal and plant cells - wikkicommons - com-mons.wikimedia.org/wiki/File:Differences_between_simple_animal_and_plant_cells_(numbers).svg

'Peacock...' - Cairomoon pixabay.com/photos/peacock-peacock-wheel-bird-animal-1706277/

'Oi Codger...' Aerobics class commons.wikimedia.org/wiki/File:Aerobics_class.jpg

'The only truths...' - Bouba/kiki effect -en.wikipedia.org/wiki/Bouba/kiki_effect

'Why do I...' - British voting map -en.wikipedia.org/wiki/2010_United_Kingdom_general_election#/media/File:2010UKElectionMap.svg

'Live in Trees' - from cover design - #squashua - instagram.com/squashua.artist/?hl=en

'Incubator' - DNA - Clker-Free-Vector-Images - pixabay.com/vectors/dna-genetic-code-double-helix-24559/

'To May' - Theresa May caricature -Donkey Hotey - commons.wikimedia.org/wiki/File:Theresa_May_-_Caricature_(41140445145).jpg

'A contrived..' Climate Chaos - Stig - shtiggy.wordpress.com/

Roses

Roses are all sorts of different colours,
violets are violet,
people say I'm pedantic
and that my poetry is well researched,
factually correct, but doesn't scan very well.

Well, try scanning this:

If it doesn't scan or you don't have a QR reader on a smartphone,
then may I recommend you download one of the latest apps?

For Android:

        en.softonic.com/solutions/apps/qr-and-barcode-scanner

For iPhone:

        itunes.apple.com/gb/app/qr-reader-for-iphone/id368494609

If you still don't know what I'm talking about, just type the web address
next to the poem titles into a web browser if you want to see what's on
the website.

If you still don't know what I'm talking about, Dad, don't worry, there
are several other people of your age who don't. You can go back to the
introduction and choose!

Enjoy!